MASTER EON'S
OFFICIAL GUIDE

APP, ZAP & SWAP!

Wherever you see this icon, you can unlock incredible free virtual content to guide you through all 256 SWAP Force combinations.

Here's how it's done . . .

Download and install the free Zappar app on your iOS or Android device*.

Open Zappar and scan the icon on the page.

Discover the SWAP Force!

*For the full list of compatible devices, log on to zappar.com/devices

EXPLORE ALL THE SKYLANDERS AND SHARE YOUR COLLECTION! DOWNLOAD THE APP NOW!

GROSSET & DUNLAP
Published by the Penguin Group
Penguin Group (USA) LLC, 375 Hudson Street, New York, New York 10014, USA

USA | Canada | UK | Ireland | Australia | New Zealand | India | South Africa | China

penguin.com
A Penguin Random House Company

ISBN 978-0-448-48060-2   10 9 8 7 6 5 4 3 2 1

MASTER EON'S
OFFICIAL GUIDE

Grosset & Dunlap
An Imprint of Penguin Group (USA) LLC

CONTENTS

WELCOME TO SKYLANDS

A NEW ADVENTURE BEGINS . . .

Greetings, Portal Master! I am Eon and I will be your guide through this book. You have opened it just in time. Skylands is in terrible danger, and only you and your Skylanders can save the day!

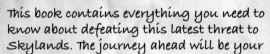

This book contains everything you need to know about defeating this latest threat to Skylands. The journey ahead will be your most challenging yet, but will bring excitement the like of which you have never seen. You will face new foes, but also meet new friends. Your quest will be full of mystery, mayhem, and more magic than you can wave an enchanted staff at!

WHAT IS SKYLANDS?

Skylands is a mystical world
of adventure and wonderment.
Made up of an infinite amount
of islands, it is protected by the
greatest group of heroes ever
known—the Skylanders.

For centuries, I guided the
Skylanders as they defended
Skylands from the evil Darkness.
Now, that task has fallen to you.
I am sure you will rise to the
challenge, with a little help from
yours truly.

But first, have you ever wondered
where all that magic comes from? Well, turn the
page to find out!

THE CLOUDBREAK ISLANDS

Of all the many islands in Skylands, many consider the Cloudbreak Islands to be the most important. Why? Because here you'll find the mighty and mystic volcano that gives the islands their name.

No other volcano explodes with such force and magnitude, which is why it was chosen by the four Ancient Elementals. Every hundred years they gather around the mouth of Mount Cloudbreak and combine their powers to create the biggest eruption possible. Waves of magic shoot out in every direction, spreading to each and every island.

ENTER THE SWAP FORCE

Realizing the importance of Mount Cloudbreak, I tasked the protection of the volcano to sixteen very special Skylanders. They oversaw the eruption ceremony for centuries, keeping the Elementals safe and ensuring the magic prospered.

Until one fateful day . . .

DID YOU KNOW?

Whenever magic is used in Skylands, a little is left over. The surplus flows back to the Cloudbreak Islands, where it is stored until the next eruption. Then, on Volcano Day, it's redistributed throughout Skylands. Clever!

INTO BATTLE!

No one knows what the Darkness truly is or where it originally came from. All we know is that it is pure evil, through and through. It longs to smother Skylands in its gloom, using the islands as a springboard to the entire universe.

On the eve of the last eruption, one hundred years ago, the servants of the Darkness attacked the Elementals. My Skylanders sprang into action.

The Skylanders won the battle, but became trapped at the summit at the exact moment of the eruption. The intense magic released by the volcano changed the Skylanders forever, granting them a unique new power. They became the SWAP Force, able to mix and match their very bodies. Each new combination brought with it unforeseen abilities. Suddenly, they had taken teamwork to a whole new level.

Now, more powerful than ever before, the SWAP Force were destined to become the greatest Skylanders of all time.

But at what cost?

TO EARTH ...
AND BACK!

The blast carried them far away from Skylands, to a tiny blue and green planet called Earth. You may know it—you are sitting on it, after all.

Thank the Elementals that you found the SWAP Force when you did, Portal Master. We are in need of their help once more. Our archenemy, Kaos, has discovered a horde of Petrified Darkness in Cloudbreak. These infernal purple crystals can be used to Evilize any living being, from the cutest animal to the bravest hero. None can resist its terrifying power.

Kaos, always looking for ways to conquer Skylands, has concocted a particularly loathsome plan. He aims to build a gigantic Evilizer in the heart of Mount Cloudbreak itself. Then, when the volcano erupts, it will spread evil far and wide. Every single being in Skylands will be Evilized. Then, Darkness will fall.

How despicable! You must master your Portal of Power and send the SWAP Force back to Skylands to stop him, before it is too late . . .

What was that? It *is* too late? Oh no! It appears that Kaos's mother has returned from wherever she has been lurking. She is so evil that she makes Kaos look like a thoroughly nice and polite individual. Hurry, Portal Master—who knows what will happen if mother and son start working together against us?

GETTING STARTED

JOURNEY INTO DANGER!

Meet Captain Flynn. He's Skylands' number-one pilot, or so he's always telling everyone. Thankfully, his heart is almost as big as his head. He has helped the Skylanders on more occasions than I can remember, and now he is standing by to assist you.

THE *DREAD-YACHT*

Flynn's beloved boat has never been the luckiest of airships. That's probably because it's cursed. Not that Flynn would ever admit there's anything wrong with the old girl. He loves her almost as much as he loves himself. And that's a lot.

Flynn was traveling to the Cloudbreak Islands to witness the eruption for himself when he was contacted by Tessa, who hails from the ancient village of Woodburrow. Her people have come under attack by minions of Kaos known as Greebles. Never able to resist a maiden in distress, Flynn has agreed to help—even though he's not too sure about her giant flying bird (known as Whiskers to its friends).

FLYNN

PERSONALITY FILE

Loyal
Conceited
Loves enchiladas
(and the ladies!)

TESSA

PERSONALITY FILE

Eager
Adventurous
A natural explorer

SKYLANDER STATS

Long ago, Kaos tried to banish the Skylanders from Skylands, transforming them into statues and exiling them to Earth. He didn't bargain on you, young Portal Master. By placing your Skylanders on a Portal of Power, you can send them back to Skylands. Kaos doesn't stand a chance!

As you guide them through their adventures, the Skylanders develop new powers and skills, becoming stronger with each new challenge. Why not try placing one on your Portal right now to check how they're progressing?

MAKE IT PERSONAL!

Look under the Quests menu to discover personalized challenges for each and every Skylander!

SKYLANDER STATS EXPLAINED

MAXIMUM HEALTH	Just how much damage your Skylander can take in battle.
SPEED	How fast they are on their feet (if they have any feet, of course!).
ARMOR	The strength of their defenses.
CRITICAL HIT	The chance of an attack inflicting more damage.
ELEMENTAL POWER	Bonus damage points they rack up in their own Elemental zones.

EON'S TIP

The more Skylanders of the same Element you add to your collection, the more their Elemental power increases.

ELEMENTS

Each of your Skylanders is also linked to one of the Elements, able to channel its power in often curious ways.

As you travel from island to island, you'll notice that certain areas favor certain Elements. Drop an Undead Skylander into an Undead area, for example, and the spooky warrior will receive more points with every battle.

THE EIGHT ELEMENTS ARE:

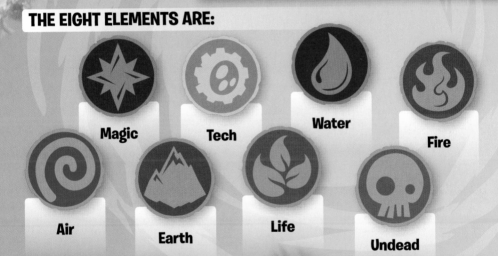

Magic

Tech

Water

Fire

Air

Earth

Life

Undead

ELEMENTAL GATES

At certain points, you may come across special gates that can only be opened by Skylanders of a certain Element. For example, Bumble Blast could buzz easily through a Life Gate, but Fryno would be left out in the cold.

Since the creation of the SWAP Force, some Elemental Gates can only be opened by a combination of Elements, such as a Skylander strong in both Undead and Tech. It's always worth exploring what lies beyond these gates. All manner of treasures can be found.

TAKE THINGS TO THE NEXT LEVEL

LEVEL UP

As you progress on your journey, your Skylanders will grow stronger. Before long, they'll start to level up. Why is this important? Well, every time they jump to a higher level, their health points increase. They'll be able to endure more damage in conflict, meaning they'll have even more chance of winning.

HOW TO LEVEL UP
See those orbs that are released every time you defeat a minion? Gobble up as many as you can to level up!

UPGRADES

Every Skylander starts with two, admittedly impressive, powers—but that is only the beginning. Collect coins, gems and treasures on your way and you'll be able to buy a host of new abilities from the Powerpods that are scattered around the islands, as well as in Woodburrow.

PORTAL MASTER RANKS

It's not only Skylanders who can level up. Leading your Skylanders into battle will also improve your Portal Master Rank. And the higher your rank, the more hats, legendary treasures, charms, and bonus missions you can purchase from Tuk in Woodburrow.

What's that? What rank am I? Why, I'm too modest to say, Portal Master. To be honest, I lost count after I reached five billion. Or was it six? I forget . . .

COLLECTIBLE ITEMS

It's not just shiny coins and sinister enemies you'll encounter on your travels. There are plenty of other trinkets to collect as well, some more useful than others.

FOOD

No one knows why there is food scattered all over Skylands. Some say it's because Hugo left the fridge open in my Citadel on the day Kaos blew up my beloved home. Whatever its origins, a quick snack after battle will restore your health.

TREASURE CHESTS

It's not just sky-pirates who like finding hidden treasure. Explore every nook and cranny of each chapter to find as many chests as you can. Give the locks a good shake and they'll soon pop off.

GIANT TREASURE CHEST

You'll need a Giant Skylander, such as Tree Rex or Crusher, to open these colossal crates. A suitably large treasure awaits within.

WINGED SAPPHIRES

Collect these sparkling winged gems whenever you can. Each one gives you a 2 percent discount on items and ability upgrades. The more you collect, the more you save.

EON'S TIP

Help Tuk set up his store and he'll reward you with a free Winged Sapphire.

23

SOUL GEMS

A Soul Gem blinks into existence every time a new Skylander is born. Not only are these precious jewels beautiful, but they unlock new abilities in the Powerpods. Hunt for as many as you can find.

STORY SCROLLS

Little nuggets of Skylands history are scattered throughout the islands. They are said to belong to Onk Beakman, Skylands' most prolific author. Judging by the fact that he's left sixteen of the things lying around, he's also Skylands' biggest litterbug.

BONUS MAPS

I'd be grateful if you could keep an eye out for these magical maps. I lent them to Flynn—who immediately lost every single one when he threw the *Dread-Yacht* into a death-defying loop-the-loop. And all so he could impress Cali. Collect them to unlock special bonus missions. You can find out more on page 160.

can find out more on page 160.

DARES

Each chapter contains special mini-dares. Chapter eight, for example, sees you searching for five rubber duckies, which I believe belong to Baron Sharpfin. The poor soul can't take his dirt-bath without them.

LEGENDARY TREASURES

DID YOU KNOW?

There are more Legendary Treasures available to buy from Tuk's Emporium! MANY more!

Tibbet, the Legendary Treasure Hunter, has dedicated his life to finding these powerful artifacts. You can't blame him. Each one boosts your Skylanders' natural abilities in a completely different way. Some of them are also quite pretty, if you like that kind of thing.

LEGENDARY TREASURE	BONUS POINTS	LOCATION
Amber Treasure	+12 Ranged Armor	Sheep Wreck Islands
Bubble Chest	+5 Gold Boost	Mudwater Hollow
Cascade Bust	+5 Elemental Strength Boost	Cascade Glade
Crooked Currency	+10 Gold Boost	Motleyville
Crystal Fire Heart	+5 Elemental Luck Boost	Twisty Tunnels
Deputee Badge	+10 Elemental Strength	Sheep Wreck Islands
Elven Arrow	+3 Critical Hit Multiplier	Winter Keep
Endless Cocoa Cup	+12 Armor	Frostfest Mountains
Epic Soap of Froth	+4 Critical Hit	Tower of Time
Expensive Souvenir	+5 Critical Hit Multiplier	Winter Keep
Geode Glide	+12 Melee Armor	Boney Islands
Glowy Mushroom	+15 Pickup Range	Fantasm Forest
Jolly Greeble	+10 Maximum Health	Iron Jaw Gulch
Luminous Lure	+10 Ranged Armor	Mudwater Hollow
Major Award Monkey	+10 Luck	Rampant Ruins
Masterful Disguise	+15 Elemental Armor Boost	Kaos's Fortress
Moltenskin Scale	+10 Elemental Food Boost	Twisty Tunnels
Mostly Magic Mirror	+5 Armor	Mount Cloudbreak
Navigator Compass	+5 Ranged Armor	Woodburrow
Skylander Scope	+2 Critical Hit Multiplier	Kaos's Fortress
The Bling Grille	+5 Elemental Food boost	Motleyville
The Brass Tap	+5 Gold Boost	Fantasm Forest
The Monkey's Paw	+5 Food Gain	Rampant Ruins
Tik-Tok Neck Clock	+10 XP Boost	Iron Jaw Gulch
Topiary of Doom	+15 Elemental Power	Fantasm Forest
Triassic Tooth	+2 Speed	Boney Islands
Urban Art	+15 XP Boost	Sheep Wreck Island
Volcano Party Pass	+10 Melee Armor	Tower of Time
Waterfall Decanter	+5 Armor	Tower of Time
Whizzing Whatsit	+30 Pickup Range	Complete 36 SWAP Zone Challenges on Nightmare Difficulty
Yeti Teddy	+5 XP Boost	Frostfest Mountains

HATS

There is an old Mabu saying that advises that if you want to get ahead, you need to get a hat. Indeed, the Skylanders love a good hat, and for a very special reason. Magical headwear can be found all over Skylands. Pop on a hat and you'll find your abilities boosted.

EON'S TIP

There are even more hats available in Tuk's Emporium in Woodburrow. Can you collect them all?

NAME	BONUS POINTS	LOCATION
Asteroid Hat	+60 Maximum Health	Kaos's Fortress
Aviator's Cap	+30 Elemental Power	Sheep Wreck Islands
Beacon Hat	+15 Elemental Power, +30 Maximum Health	Frostfest Mountains
Beanie Hat	+5 Speed, +20 Elemental Power	Tower of Time
Bearskin Hat	+5 Critical Hit, +10 Elemental Power, +10 Maximum Health	Boney Islands
Boater Hat	+3 Speed, +20 Maximum Health	Mudwater Hollow
Boonie Hat	+10 Elemental Power, +10 Maximum Health	Rampant Ruins
Capuchon	+20 Armor, +10 Maximum Health	Motleyville
Creepy Helm	+15 Armor, +9 Critical Hit	Sheep Wreck Islands
Crown of Frost	+30 Armor	Winter Keep
Fishbone Hat	+9 Speed, +7 Critical Hit	Boney Islands
Flower Garland	+10 Critical Hit	Fantasm Forest
Four Winds Hat	+15 Speed	Frostfest Mountains
Gaucho Hat	+10 Armor, +10 Elemental Power, +10 Maximum Health	Iron Jaw Gulch

NAME	BONUS POINTS	LOCATION
Glittering Tiara	+6 Speed, +2 Critical Hit. +10 Maximum Health	Cascade Glade
Greeble Hat	+20 Maximum Health	Mount Cloudbreak
Leprechaun Hat	+5 Armor, +2 Critical Hit, +10 Maximum Health	Tower of Time
Life Preserver Hat	+30 Maximum Health	Mount Cloudbreak
Peacock Hat	+10 Armor, +10 Elemental Power, +10 Maximum Health	Twisty Tunnels
Puma Hat	+10 Armor, +2 Critical Hit. +10 Elemental Power	Woodburrow
Rain Hat	+7 Armor, +2 Critical Hit	Cascade Glade
Roundlet	+5 Armor, +5 Elemental Power, +20 Maximum Health	Motleyville
Sawblade Hat	+7 Critical Hit, +5 Elemental Power	Rampant Ruins
Ski Cap	+6 Speed, +30 Maximum Health	Winter Keep
Stone Hat	+5 Armor, +7 Critical Hit	Mudwater Hollow
Stovepipe Hat	+5 Armor, +2 Critical Hit, +5 Elemental Power	Mount Cloudbreak
The Outsider	+8 Maximum Health, +7 Elemental Power	Cascade Glade
Tree Branch	+30 Maximum Health, +7 Critical Hit	Sheep Wreck Islands
Tricorn Hat	+15 Armor, +2 Critical Hit	Twisty Tunnels
Turkey Hat	+50 Maximum Health	Woodburrow
UFO Hat	+40 Maximum Health, +9 Speed, +15 Elemental Power	Place UFO Magic Item on Portal
Volcano Hat	+50 Maximum Health, +15 Speed, +25 Armor	Complete Story Mode on Nightmare Difficulty
Zombeanie	+40 Maximum Health	Iron Jaw Gulch

WELCOME TO WOODBURROW

Woodburrow is a charming place, nestling in the shadow of Mount Cloudbreak. I spent a wonderful vacation here once. It must have been five hundred years ago now. The place hasn't changed a bit.

EON'S TIP
Can you find your way up to Treetrunk Peak? It might be worth taking a hive dive...

RUFUS

The village crier is the first person you'll meet when you enter Woodburrow. He always knows what's what. If you get stuck, pop over to Rufus in the Central Plaza. He'll point you in the right direction.

THE POWERPOD

Gorm is the protector of the Powerpod, a magical device that can upgrade your Skylander—for the right price. You should also make use of Gorm's training grounds. Whack one of his training dummies to see how much punch your Skylanders are packing.

EON'S TIP

Clamber up the Mushroom Stairway near the Air Docks. You'll find an extra hidden treat!

TUK'S EMPORIUM

Help Tuk, Gorm's brother, to set up shop and he will sell you all manner of items to help you on your adventures. Hats, Legendary Treasures, Bonus Mission Maps, charms—they're all here.

THE TROPHY ROOM

When you can, head to the Trophy Room to meet Tibbet, the Legendary Treasure Hunter. He'll point out the pedestals that are dotted around Woodburrow. These come in handy when you start collecting Legendary Treasures. Pop the treasures on the pedestals and they'll start boosting your abilities right away.

THE GREAT HOLLOW

Located in the great fershlupping tree, the Great Hollow is home to Woodburrow's council. You'll also find a couple of magic Treasure Chests. The Yeti Councillor's chest can only be opened using a Skylander matching the Element shown on its lid.

SPARK LOCKS

Spark Locks can be found all over Cloudbreak Islands, including on the Gillman Councillor's chest. You'll need to bring Shock and Bolt together to spring the lock. Getting the two bright sparks past the grid's tricky obstacles is tougher than it looks.

THE UNDER HOLLOW

Wheellock the Dirt Shark has supplied a special fishing rod to help you unwind. Head to the Under Hollow to relax. Just watch out for those electric eels.

EXTRA

Just what is behind that gate in the Hollow? You'll need Skylanders of more than one Element to find out.

THE **RUSTY BASS**
BAIT SHOPPE

EON'S TIP

You might just
want to check up
by the main
village gates,
Portal Master.

MEET THE SWAP FORCE

HOOT LOOP

"LET'S RUFFLE SOME FEATHERS!"

A night at the circus turned out to be more spectacular than expected when I witnessed the Amazing Hoot Loop single-handedly defeat a horde of Greebles. I made him a Skylander there and then.

SOUL GEM
in Woodburrow

WAND OF DREAMS Shoot three Déjàbooms at once.

INFINITE LOOP Release your ring beneath Hoot Loop to cause serious shockwaves.

STARTING STATS		**PERSONALITY** FILE
Max Health	250	**Master magician**
Speed	43	**Born performer**
Armor	12	**Always on the move**
Critical Hit	6	**Trickster**
Elemental Power	25	

SPECIAL QUEST

WOULD YOU LIKE TO PLAY A GAME? Defeat 50 enemies with the final explosion of the Flashback attack.

Starting Power

Attack 1

DÉJÀBOOM! Your magic projectile blasts enemies three times before disappearing.

Power Upgrades

300 Gold

HYPNOTISM Mesmerize your foes to slow them right down.

800 Gold

TRICKED YA! Get shiny new magic armor.

1,000 Gold

FLASHBACK Your Déjàboom becomes a bouncing bomb.

"Choose Your Path" Upgrades

Path 1: Dream-Weaver
Build Hoot Loot's beams

1500 Gold

DREAM BEAM Throw a devastating dream beam.

2000 Gold

BAD DREAMS BEAM Make your Dream Beam badder.

Path 2: Hypno-Owl
Heap power into Hoot Loop's hypnosis

1,500 Gold

MASS HYPNOSIS Spread your charm over a wider area.

2,000 Gold

DEEP ASLEEP Hyped-up hypnosis is yours.

Starting Power

Attack 2

LOOP THE LOOP! Teleport forward a short distance, damaging your foes.

Power Upgrades

300 Gold

PORTABLE HOLE Aim your teleportation ring.

800 Gold

TEMPORAL WHACK Teleporting damages more enemies.

1,000 Gold

TIME SINK Pull enemies and objects to your teleportation ring.

"Choose Your Path" Upgrades

Path 1: Telekinesis
More teleportation tweaks

1,500 Gold

NOW YOU SEE ME Charge your ring to do more damage.

2,000 Gold

COMPLETE CONCENTRATION Make a more impressive entrance.

Path 2: Escape Artist
Teleportation to the max

1,500 Gold

NOW YOU DON'T Nip back to your original position.

2,000 Gold

TELEPORT TURBULENCE Max damage on all teleportation effects.

TRAP SHADOW

"HIDE AND SLEEK!"

Hunting legend Trap Shadow was captured by a group of wizards who wanted to use him to ensnare me! The nerve! Thankfully, he used his considerable skills against my would-be abductors.

SOUL GEM
in Frostfest Mountains

SHADOW STRIKER Unleash a shadow dash during claw attacks.

LIVING SHADOW Turn invisible as you prowl.

STARTING STATS		PERSONALITY FILE
Max Health	270	Sneaky
Speed	43	Cunning
Armor	12	Ingenious
Critical Hit	8	Patient
Elemental Power	25	

SPECIAL QUEST

OH SNAP! Defeat 50 enemies with your traps.

Starting Power

Attack 1

CLAWING SHADOW Swipe enemies with your claws.

Power Upgrades

300 Gold

SNAP TRAP Throw traps to capture foes.

800 Gold

SHARP MAGIC Perform powerful claw attacks.

1,000 Gold

CATCH! Throw a quick Snap Trap.

"Choose Your Path" Upgrades

Path 1: Feral Instincts
Give your kitty some claws!

1,500 Gold

ME-OUCH! Swipe enemies into the air.

2,000 Gold

NOCTURNAL PREDATOR Me-Ouch with even more Ouch!

Path 2: Trap Trickster
Add some explosive oomph to your traps

1,500 Gold

GLOOM AND BOOM Traps go bang!

2,000 Gold

MAKE IT SNAPPY! All traps are more powerful.

Starting Power

Attack 2

SHADOW KICK Deliver a killer kick!

Power Upgrades

300 Gold

PROWL Enemies you touch while prowling get pummelled.

800 Gold

NINE LIVES Increase your health in hairy moments.

1,000 Gold

OUT OF THE SHADOWS Your prowl ends in an explosion.

"Choose Your Path" Upgrades

Path 1: Shadow Combat
Give your kicks a kick

1,500 Gold

DARK MAGIC The force of your kick is felt farther away.

2,000 Gold

BLACK CAT Shadow waves become more shocking.

Path 2: Prowler
Pep-up Trap Shadow's prowl!

1,500 Gold

SHADE STEPS Leave poisonous paw prints when you prowl.

2,000 Gold

BUMPS IN THE NIGHT Super-strength Shade Steps.

FREEZE BLADE

"KEEPING IT COOL!"

When Freeze Blade helped save Blast Zone from Spell Punks, Blast was so grateful that he recommended the speedy skater to me as a potential Skylander.

SOUL GEM
in Fantasm Forest

WINTER CHAKRAM Increased critical hit chance and damage are yours.

ICEBERG ENDURANCE Dash through attacks.

STARTING STATS

Max Health	280
Speed	50
Armor	6
Critical Hit	8
Elemental Power	25

PERSONALITY FILE

Versatile
Slick
Smooth
Sharp-witted

SPECIAL QUEST

CHILL OUT FOR A SECOND Freeze 100 enemies with Frostcicles.

Starting Power

Attack 1

CHAKRAM THROW Chuck a chilly chakram.

Power Upgrades

300 Gold

FROSTCICLE Fire ice bolts that freeze your foes.

800 Gold

ICICLES Give your chakrams icy armor.

1,000 Gold

FRIGID WHIRL Charge up your chakram before throwing.

"Choose Your Path" Upgrades

Path 1: Blizzard Blade Path
Chakram masterclasses!

1,500 Gold

SHAVED ICE A charged chakram shoots ice everywhere.

2,000 Gold

WHITEOUT Ice from a chakram does more damage.

Path 2: Ice Sculptor Path
Boost Freeze Blade's Frostcicles

1,500 Gold

OH SNOW! Charge your Frosticles to bring a deep freeze.

2,000 Gold

ICE TO MEET YOU Frostcicle and Oh Snow! get amped up.

Starting Power

Attack 2

SPEEDY SKATE Slip ahead of the opposition.

Power Upgrades

300 Gold

ICE TRAIL Slow enemies with your snowy slipstream.

800 Gold

GLACIAL COAT Get ice-cool armor.

1000 Gold

BLADED BUTTERFLY Pull off a trick that leaves enemies reeling.

"Choose Your Path" Upgrades

Path 1: Trail Freezer
Leave your enemies cold

1,500 Gold

FLASH FREEZE Your ice trail does serious damage.

2,000 Gold

NICE ICE Flash Freeze gets cooler still.

Path 2: Ice Skater
Puts evil on ice!

1,500 Gold

PENALTY FROST Enemies explode in damaging ice patches.

2,000 Gold

ICED SKATES Penalty Frost gets stronger.

WASH BUCKLER

"EIGHT LEGS AND NO PEGS!"

Never one for the pirating way of life, this Mermasquid convinced his swashbuckling shipmates to switch to more heroic pastimes.

 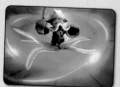
STARTING STATS

Max Health	270
Speed	43
Armor	24
Critical Hit	8
Elemental Power	25

PERSONALITY FILE

Noble
Persuasive
Multi tasker
Commanding

SPECIAL QUEST

SLEEP WITH THE FISHES Defeat 50 foes with fish-filled bubbles.

Starting Power

Attack 1

SWORD SLASH Swing your watery weapon.

Power Upgrades

300 Gold

BUBBLE BLASTER Trap baddies in bubbles.

800 Gold

BLADESAIL Charge up your cutlass for a crazy dash.

1,000 Gold

DANGEROUS WATERS Shoot piranha-filled bubbles. Snap snap!

"Choose Your Path" Upgrades

Path 1: Cutlass Captain
Soup up your sword

1,500 Gold

PARLEY POPPER Create a bubble shield.

2,000 Gold

FIRST MATE CUTLASS Sword Slashes cause more damage.

Path 2: Bubble Buccaneer
You're forever blowing bubbles

1,500 Gold

MAROONED Release not one but two bubbles.

2,000 Gold

CAPTAIN OF PIRANHA BAY Piranhas have more bites.

Starting Power

Attack 2

SOMERSAULT Roll over enemies with your tentacles.

Power Upgrades

300 Gold

OCTOLASH Slap enemies with your tentacles.

800 Gold

DEEP SKIN Your health gets a booty bonus.

1,000 Gold

INK JET Cover enemies in inky blackness.

"Choose Your Path" Upgrades

Path 1: Tentacoolest
Tune up your tentacles

1500 Gold

TENTACLEAVER Repeatedly slap your enemies.

2,000 Gold

SEA LEGS Tentacles have never been so powerful.

Path 2: Ink Artist Path
If you think that ink is the thing

1,500 Gold

INK TRAIL You leave behind a cloud of ink.

2,000 Gold

THIS WILL NEVER COME OUT! Ink attacks leave enemies black 'n' blue.

MAGNA CHARGE

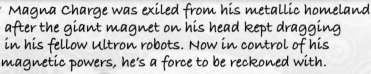

"ATTRACT TO ATTACK!"

Magna Charge was exiled from his metallic homeland after the giant magnet on his head kept dragging in his fellow Ultron robots. Now in control of his magnetic powers, he's a force to be reckoned with.

SOUL GEM
in Mount Cloudbreak

MULTIBARRELLED Magnet Cannons fire three blasts, not one.

SUPER REPULSOR Wheel a little "tired"? Get a new and improved one, then!

STARTING STATS

Max Health	280
Speed	50
Armor	18
Critical Hit	6
Elemental Power	25

PERSONALITY FILE

Military-minded
Strong-willed
Always in a rush
Attractive!

SPECIAL QUEST

NOW THAT'S USING YOUR HEAD Cause 5,000 damage with your Polarized Pickup.

Starting Power

Attack 1

MAGNET CANNON
Fire energy projectiles, but be careful not to overheat.

Power Upgrades

300 Gold

POLARIZED PICKUP Grab and slam enemies with your magnet.

800 Gold

PLASMA SHOTS Rapid-fire heat missiles are yours.

1,000 Gold

MAGNETIC BUILDUP Use Polarized Pickup for extra damage.

"Choose Your Path" Upgrades

Path 1: Magnetic Armaments
Get a mega Magnet Cannon!

1,500 Gold

DISCHARGE RECHARGE Overheat your Magnet Cannon for fireballs.

2,000 Gold

HEAVY BLASTER Fireballs blaze brighter.

Path 2: Magnet Tuner
Your pickups get powered up

1,500 Gold

BURST PICKUP Polarized Pickup repels enemies.

2,000 Gold

MAGNETIC PERSONALITY Magnet attacks ramp up more damage.

Starting Power

Attack 2

MAGNETO BALL Drag small enemies with you.

Power Upgrades

300 Gold

EJECT Throw enemies while dragging.

800 Gold

RAD WHEELS Get a speed boost.

1,000 Gold

DRAG CAPACITY Drag two enemies at once.

"Choose Your Path" Upgrades

Path 1: Static Buildup
Become a bigger drag than usual!

1,500 Gold

SHOCK STOP Give your dragged enemies a big shock.

2,000 Gold

CRASH TEST Shock Stop and Eject cause more damage.

Path 2: Drag Racer Path
Life can be such a drag

1,500 Gold

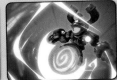

RAPID REPEL Shoot dragged enemies without stopping.

2,000 Gold

OPPOSITES REPEL Rapid Repel gets more repulsive.

SPY RISE

"IT'S CLASSIFIED!"

I knew I wanted this scuttling private investigator on the case when it came to protecting all of Skylands.

SOUL GEM
in Boney Islands

SPY WITH A GOLDEN HAND
Get a golden blaster that packs five shots at once.

OMEGA SKY LASER Shoot a laser from your web.

Starting Power

Attack 1

SPYDER BLASTER Shoot a trio of Spyder projectiles to slow down bad guys.

Power Upgrades

300 Gold

SUPER SPY SCANNER S3 Scan for nearby enemies and then shoot a top secret laser.

800 Gold

SPYDER STING Steal health from your enemies.

1,000 Gold

FUTURE TECH Give your Spy Scanner and Spyder Blaster a boost.

"Choose Your Path" Upgrades

Path 1: Web Spinner
Make Spy Rise a webbed wonder!

1,500 Gold

COCOON SPINNER Cover your enemies in sticky web.

2,000 Gold

EXPERIMENTAL WEB Your cocoons inflict more damage.

Path 2: Shock Spy
Bug Bombs-a-go-go

1,500 Gold

ELECTROWEB PULSE BOMB Charge and chuck a web explosive.

2,000 Gold

IMPROVE EPB A bigger web blast can be yours.

Starting Power

Attack 2

SPYDER CLIMB Climb up electrowebs to drop down on enemies.

Power Upgrades

300 Gold

SPYDER MINE Drop homing Spyder mines from above.

800 Gold

SPYDER MINE 002 Drop two Spyder mines for double the damage.

1,000 Gold

RAPID LASER LEGS V17 Energy bolts—for four legs only.

"Choose Your Path" Upgrades

Path 1: Fire Tech
Give Spy Rise's feet a little extra kick

1,500 Gold

FOOT-MOUNTED FLAME Fire flames from your feet.

2,000 Gold

BLUE FLAME Feet flames get hotter.

Path 2: Electro Tech
Power up your Pulse Cannons!

1,500 Gold

PULSE CANNON Laser bolts get an extra charge.

2,000 Gold

ADVANCED PULSE CANNON New and improved pulses.

GRILLA DRILLA

"IF THERE'S A DRILL, THERE'S A WAY!"

Grilla Drilla was declared heir to the Drilla Empire after saving the Drilla king from trolls—but he gave it all up to become a Skylander.

RING OF THE GOLDEN MONKEY
Golden arm drills pack more punch

ADAPTIVE NATURE Planted Turrets become thorny problems

STARTING STATS		PERSONALITY FILE
Max Health	290	Dauntless
Speed	43	Rugged
Armor	24	No-nonsense
Critical Hit	4	Honor-bound
Elemental Power	25	

SPECIAL QUEST

MONKEYS MEAN BUSINESS Use summoned monkeys to inflict a total of 2,000 damage.

Starting Power

Attack 1

PUNCHY MONKEY Simian-slam nearby enemies.

Power Upgrades

300 Gold

MONKEY CALL Summon two crazed monkeys.

800 Gold

SILVERBACK Your punches get more power.

1,000 Gold

REACHING MANDRILL Fighting fists reach farther.

"Choose Your Path" Upgrades

Path 1: Monkey Master Path
Go bananas with your monkey attacks

1,500 Gold

TEAM MONKEY Summon four monkeys instead of two.

2,000 Gold

KING OF THE JUNGLE Your monkey mob makes more mayhem.

Path 2: Drilling Punches
Grilla Drilla's punches get pepped up

1,500 Gold

DOUBLE PUNCH Use both drills to punch bad guys.

2,000 Gold

PRIMATE POWER Double Punch gets double the power.

Starting Power

Attack 2

PLANTED TURRET Coconut turrets target enemies.

Power Upgrades

300 Gold

EXPLOSIVE GROWTH Turrets release explosive plants.

800 Gold

SPREADING LIKE WEEDS Exploding plants seed three more bombs.

1,000 Gold

NATURE'S BOUNTY Plant a bigger crop of coconut turrets.

"Choose Your Path" Upgrades

Path 1: Coconut Caretaker
Your turrets go completely nuts

1,500 Gold

THIS IS COCONUTS! Turret projectiles go boom.

2,000 Gold

COCONUT MAYHEM Nutty explosions are now better than ever.

Path 2: Banana Blaster Path
No chance of slipping up here!

1,500 Gold

BANANA SPLIT What's better than coconuts? Bananas!

2,000 Gold

GO BANANAS! Banana Turrets to the max.

STINK BOMB

"CLEAR THE AIR!"

As soon as I got a sniff of this young ninja and his mastery of Skunk-Fu, I knew I had to have him on my team—no matter how much he reeked!

SOUL GEM
in Winter Keep

MASTER-STAR TECHNIQUE
Upgrade your store of Skunk-Fu Stars.

STEALTH SKUNK Stay invisible even after attacking enemies.

STARTING STATS

Max Health	270
Speed	43
Armor	12
Critical Hit	6
Elemental Power	25

PERSONALITY FILE

Kicks up a stink!
Mysterious
Bit of a loner
Dedicated

SPECIAL QUEST

WHAT'S THAT SMELL? Stink out 50 enemies using your One-Inch Palm.

Starting Power
Attack 1

SKUNK-FU STARS Throw stinking stars.

Power Upgrades

300 Gold

800 Gold

1,000 Gold

ONE-INCH PALM Deliver a powerful palm punch.

NOXIOUS NINJA Stars cause serious damage.

SWEEPING SKUNK-FU Throw stars by the handful.

"Choose Your Path" Upgrades

Path 1: The Art of Skunk-Fu
Freshen up your shooting stars!

1,500 Gold

2,000 Gold

SKUNK-FU SHIELD Create a shield of Skunk-Fu Stars.

SKUNK-FU MASTER Your shield gets super-strong.

Path 2: The Art of Acorns
From tiny acorns grow . . .

1,500 Gold

2,000 Gold

ACORN ACCURACY Charge and fire a poison acorn dart.

SKUNK EYE Acorn attacks grow in power.

Starting Power
Attack 2

SKUNK CLOUD Shroud yourself in an invisible stink.

Power Upgrades

300 Gold

800 Gold

1,000 Gold

HIDDEN TAIL Attack with your tail while unseen.

SPORTING STRIPES Invisible attacks become swifter.

SKUNKING AROUND Leave a bad smell that makes your foes sick.

"Choose Your Path" Upgrades

Path 1: Skunk Cloud Controller
Clouds become more potent!

1,500 Gold

2,000 Gold

ROLLING FOG Two Skunk Clouds are smellier than one.

CLOUDY CONCOCTION Super-stinky Skunk Cloud action.

Path 2: Sneaky Tricks
Time to get sneakier!

1,500 Gold

2,000 Gold

SNEAKY TACTICS Drop pointy stars to slow opponents.

PAIN IN THE FOOT Sneaking Action gets even sneakier.

NIGHT SHIFT

"ROLL WITH THE PUNCHES!"

This Batcrypt phantomweight found himself disqualified from boxing when teleportation was banned in the rules—but he still gets to use his skills on the forces of Darkness.

STARTING STATS

Max Health	200
Speed	35
Armor	4
Critical Hit	8
Elemental Power	25

PERSONALITY FILE

Charming
Refined
Sporting
A real knockout

SPECIAL QUEST

KING OF THE RING Hit 10 enemies with one giant uppercut punch.

SOUL GEM
in Motleyville

GENTLEMANLY All attacks deliver more damage at full health.

GRAND ENTRANCE Enemies slow down when you teleport.

Starting Power

Attack 1

ONE-TWO PUNCH
Deliver a blow to nearby enemies.

Power Upgrades

300 Gold

VAMPIRE'S BITE Nip enemies to gain health.

800 Gold

STING LIKE A BAT Punching does more damage.

1,000 Gold

DON'T MOVE, JUST STICK! Charge a punch before throwing it.

"Choose Your Path" Upgrades

Path 1: Proper Vampire
Fangs for the upgrades!

1,500 Gold

INFECTIOUS SMILE Vampire's Bite drains health for longer.

2,000 Gold

HEALTHY APPETITE Take even more health.

Path 2: Champion Fighter
Earn bigger rewards!

1,500 Gold

PRIZE FIGHTER Punched enemies drop money. Ka-ching!

2,000 Gold

PAYDAY More cash with every uppercut.

Starting Power

Attack 2

ETHEREAL SHIFT
Teleport forward.

Power Upgrades

300 Gold

FLOAT LIKE A VAMPIRE Shoot projectiles while teleporting.

800 Gold

FOGGY MOVEMENT Your smoke form gets speedier.

1,000 Gold

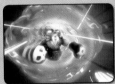

A BATTY COACH A bat buddy prevents you being defeated one time only.

"Choose Your Path" Upgrades

Path 1: Warping Vortex
Who said Kaos has the monopoly on doom?

1,500 Gold

VORTEX OF DOOM Your teleportation effect pulls in enemies.

2,000 Gold

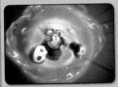

CLOSE TO DOOM Your Vortex gets a little more va-va-dooooom.

Path 2: Underbat
Battered bat coaches are more useful

1,500 Gold

ROUND 2 Your bat coach gives you a health boost.

2,000 Gold

LUCK OF THE UNDERBAT Bat Coach can be used twice.

RATTLE SHAKE

"GO AHEAD—SNAKE MY DAY!"

This sharpshooter can summon serpents from all sides—as the infamous Black Hat Cowboy Gang found out when they tried to trick him into helping them raid Mount Cloudbreak.

STARTING STATS

Max Health	280
Speed	43
Armor	12
Critical Hit	8
Elemental Power	25

PERSONALITY FILE

Cocky
Dauntless
Sure shot
Ssslithery

SPECIAL QUEST

BOUNCING BITER Damage 100 foes with Spring-Loaded Snakes.

SOUL GEM
in Cascade Glade

RAISE THE SNAKES Slip into a comfortable, ability-boosting skin.

THE SNAKE-SKINNED KID Become a speedy snake sprinter.

Starting Power

Attack 1

SNAKE'S VENOM Shoot snake venom at enemies.

Power Upgrades

300 Gold

DEPUTY SNAKE A slippery sidekick attacks nearby baddies.

800 Gold

FISTFUL OF SNAKES Venom projectiles have more bite.

1,000 Gold

SPRING-LOADED SNAKE Charged serpents ricochet between enemies.

"Choose Your Path" Upgrades

Path 1: Deputy's Duty
Give your Deputy a boost

1,500 Gold

NASTY SSSURPRISE Deputy Snake explodes with acid.

2,000 Gold

ARMED TO THE FANGS Nasty Sssurprises get nastier.

Path 2: Coiled Ammunition
Put venom into Spring-Loaded bites

1,500 Gold

SNAKE BITE Spring-Loaded Snake poisons its first victim.

2,000 Gold

THIS BITES Poisoned enemies feel even worse.

Starting Power

Attack 2

TAIL SWEEP Tail attacks rattle nearby enemies.

Power Upgrades

300 Gold

BOUNCE THE BONES Bouncing bony fangs are released.

800 Gold

ON BRAND Bounce up and down on enemies.

1,000 Gold

SSSTAMPEDE Three bone projectiles are yours.

"Choose Your Path" Upgrades

Path 1: Bone Herder
Snakes alive, that's a big serpent!

1,500 Gold

GOLIATH BONE SNAKE The biggest snake skeleton your enemies have ever seen.

2,000 Gold

DANCES WITH SNAKES Release more than one bone snake at a time.

Path 2: Grave Springer Path
Things are looking grave for evil

1,500 Gold

SPURRED SPRINGS Super-charge Sssstampede.

2,000 Gold

GRAVEYARD SMASH Drop gravestones on your foes.

RUBBLE ROUSER

"BRACE FOR IMPACT!"

While his fellow miners ate their way through rock, Rubble Rouser preferred using a hammer or drill. How they mocked—until he hammered the evil Rock Lords who tried to conquer their mountain.

SOUL GEM
in Winter Keep

OBSIDIAN SKIN Your skin becomes rock hard.

POP ROCK The biggest boulder attack of all.

STARTING STATS

Max Health	280
Speed	35
Armor	24
Critical Hit	6
Elemental Power	25

PERSONALITY FILE

Inventive
Imaginative
Open to new ideas
Trustworthy

SPECIAL QUEST

OH, WHAT A DRILL! Cause 400 damage in one drill-fuelled earthquake.

Starting Power

Attack 1

HAMMER SWING Charge up your massive two-headed hammer.

Power Upgrades

300 Gold

TOOLS OF THE TRADE Smash nearby enemies with your hammer.

800 Gold

HAPPY HAMMERING Hammer attacks get more hammery.

1000 Gold

DRILL HEAD Drill into the ground to cause an earthquake.

"Choose Your Path" Upgrades

Path 1: Drill Pitcher
It's hammer time!

1,500 Gold

NAILED IT! Chuck your charged hammer!

2,000 Gold

SLEDGEHAMMER Thrown hammers cause more calamity.

Path 2: Excavator Path
Beware low-flying shrapnel

1,500 Gold

ROCK SHARDS Hammer blows create deadly shrapnel.

2,000 Gold

GEM QUALITY Deliver super-sized shards.

Starting Power

Attack 2

DEEP DIG Dive underground to surprise enemies.

Power Upgrades

300 Gold

MINOR MINERS Summon mini-miners to help your fight.

800 Gold

EARTHY FORTITUDE Get a health boost.

1,000 Gold

TUNNEL EXPEDITION Underground attacks go over the top.

"Choose Your Path" Upgrades

Path 1: Bolder Boulders
Unleash a tunnel of terror!

1,500 Gold

BOULDER TOSS Aim boulders at enemies while tunneling.

2,000 Gold

SO BOLD Boulders come down harder.

Path 2: Miner Foreman
Bolster your merry band of miners

1,500 Gold

MINER CRAFT Four miners at your command.

2,000 Gold

ON STRIKE Not so minor miners any more.

DOOM STONE

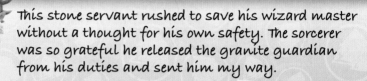

This stone servant rushed to save his wizard master without a thought for his own safety. The sorcerer was so grateful he released the granite guardian from his duties and sent him my way.

SOUL GEM
in Kaos's Fortress

STONEY STARE Enchanted snakes come alive on your shield.

SPIN THE TABLES Your fourth spin gets even bigger!

STARTING STATS		PERSONALITY FILE
Max Health	280	Happy to help
Speed	35	Optimistic
Armor	30	Self-sacrificing
Critical Hit	6	Skilled stone fighter
Elemental Power	25	

SPECIAL QUEST

STOP HITTING YOURSELF Defeat 50 Chompies by blocking alone.

Starting Power

Attack 1

COLUMN CLUB Clobber creeps with your column.

Power Upgrades

300 Gold

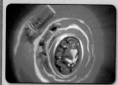

LIVING STATUE Block close attacks, leaving enemies stunned.

800 Gold

REJECT AND REFLECT Deflect projectiles to turn enemies into jade.

1000 Gold

COLUMN DUTY Charge your column to cause more damage.

"Choose Your Path" Upgrades

Path 1: Column Clubber
Build a better column

1,500 Gold

FALLING TO PIECES Your column splits to cover a larger area.

2,000 Gold

CLUB DOOM Charge that column for longer.

Path 2: Jaded Fighter
Leave your foes jaded!

1,500 Gold

CRACKING UP Enemies turned to jade will shoot shards at others!

2,000 Gold

MORE DORIC WARFARE Blocked attacks deal more damage to attackers.

BOTTOM

Starting Power

Attack 2

STONY SPIN A quick charge unleashes a big stone belt.

Power Upgrades

300 Gold

SPIN RIGHT AROUND Bounce between enemies.

800 Gold

REVOLUTIONARY BELT Spins cause more damage.

1,000 Gold

SPEEDY SPINNER Spin faster to go faster.

"Choose Your Path" Upgrades

Path 1: Serious Spinner
Become a spinball wizard

1,500 Gold

THE HARDER THEY FALL The last victim of your spin shoots into the air.

2,000 Gold

SPINBALL KING Spin Right Around gets a boost.

Path 2: Carved Belt
Boost your belt spins

1,500 Gold

JADED SPIN Jade projectiles shoot from spinning belts.

2,000 Gold

BELT PELTERS Projectiles get more powerful.

BOOM JET

"BOMBS AWAY!"

When the Darkness descended on his hometown, sky surfer Boom Jet raced from house to house saving his neighbors. After making sure everyone was safe, he flew straight to me to offer his services.

SOUL GEM
in Motleyville

SUPPLY DROP Air Strike can drop health if needed.

MACH 2 A blast damages enemies at the beginning of a dash.

STARTING STATS

Max Health	260
Speed	43
Armor	24
Critical Hit	6
Elemental Power	25

PERSONALITY FILE

Daredevil
Hyperactive
Brave
Competitive

SPECIAL QUEST

TACTICAL STRIKES Defeat 747 enemies using Air Strikes.

Starting Power

Attack 1

FOOTBALL BOMB Hut 1. Hut 2. Hut 3. *BOOM!*

Power Upgrades

300 Gold

AIR STRIKE Bombs drop from the sky.

800 Gold

TIGHT SPIRAL Football bombs cause bigger bangs.

1000 Gold

GO LONG! Charge up a mega Football Bomb.

"Choose Your Path" Upgrades

Path 1: Storm Bomber
Become an Air Strike Ace

1,500 Gold

STORM BOMB Bombs cause storm clouds when they land.

2,000 Gold

UNFRIENDLY SKIES Storm Bombs get stormier.

Path 2: Squad Leader
Boost your Storm Bombs!

1,500 Gold

BOMBERS Bomb larger areas from above.

2,000 Gold

TIGHT FORMATION Air Strikes strike harder.

Starting Power

Attack 2

WIND TURBINE Wind pushes enemies back.

Power Upgrades

300 Gold

MACH 1 Dash forward.

800 Gold

ACE PILOT Dash forward faster.

1,000 Gold

TURBULENCE Homing propellers away!

"Choose Your Path" Upgrades

Path 1: Sky Writer
Smoke those enemies out

1,500 Gold

SKY WRITING Enemies get stung by your trail.

2,000 Gold

THICK SMOKE Foes eat your smoke for longer.

Path 2: Ace Gunner
Set your sites on a new flyer

1,500 Gold

GUN SHIP Get a missile-firing flyer.

2,000 Gold

ROCKET FUEL Your flyer gets more impressive missiles.

FREE RANGER

"WHIP UP A STORM!"

I rescued this storm-hunting rooster just as he was about to jump into the Darkness itself. He soon saw that fighting evil was more exciting than extreme weather.

STARTING STATS

Max Health	280
Speed	43
Armor	18
Critical Hit	8
Elemental Power	25

PERSONALITY FILE

Thrill-seeker
Bold
Impulsive
Hasty

SPECIAL QUEST

RUFFLED FEATHERS Wallop enemies 25 times without stopping melee attacks.

SOUL GEM
in Mudwater Hollow

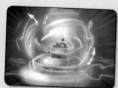

STORMING STORMBLADES Stormblades get lightning-charged.

CHARGED WINDS Fill your tornados with lightning.

Starting Power

Attack 1

STORMBLADE SLASH Slash with those super-sharp Stormblades.

Power Upgrades

300 Gold

EYES OF THE STORM Unleash your lightning vision.

800 Gold

CHARGED BLADES An even more storming Stormblade attack.

1,000 Gold

GALE SLASH Send out shockwaves of solid air.

"Choose Your Path" Upgrades

Path 1: Wind Slasher
Super-charge your storms

1,500 Gold

SLICING STORM Charge and release a Stormblade combo.

2,000 Gold

FEATHERED FURY Slicing Storms get darker still.

Path 2: Storm Focus Path
If looks could thrill . . .

1,500 Gold

LIGHTNING STRIKES THRICE Your electrifying gaze gets stronger.

2,000 Gold

CHARGED GIGAWATT BOLT Strike up even more of a lightning storm.

Starting Power

Attack 2

RIDE THE WIND Twist into a tornado of terror.

Power Upgrades

300 Gold

APPROACHING STORM Your twister gets turbocharged.

800 Gold

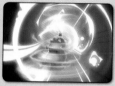

WIND POWERED Tornadoes twist for longer.

1,000 Gold

TORNADO VACUUM BOOST Your tornadoes suck more enemies in!

"Choose Your Path" Upgrades

Path 1: Lightning Linguist
Electrify your twisters!

1,500 Gold

LIGHTNING NOVA Add lightning to your tornadoes.

2,000 Gold

NOVA FLASH Make that lightning more striking.

Path 2: Tornado Thrower Path
Tornadoes get enemies in a twist

1,500 Gold

WILD TORNADO Your tornado spawns another twister.

2,000 Gold

TWISTED TWISTER Cause even more storm damage.

BLAST ZONE

Fed up with Blast Zone defusing their bombs, trolls threw a load of them down the Furnace Knight's chimney. He simply swallowed the lot and belched a stream of fire at his attackers. Awesome!

SOUL GEM
in Fantasm Forest

BOMB PARTY Throw two bombs at a time.

HOT FEET Leave a trail of fire when you're dashing.

STARTING STATS		PERSONALITY FILE
Max Health	290	Explosive
Speed	43	Volatile
Armor	24	Valiant
Critical Hit	6	Relentless
Elemental Power	25	

SPECIAL QUEST

IF YOU CAN'T STAND THE HEAT Take out 10 enemies with one Flame Breath.

Attack 1
Starting Power

BOMB THROW Lob a bomb at enemies.

Power Upgrades

300 Gold	800 Gold	1,000 Gold

FLAME BREATH Create a wall of fire while turning.

POWER BOMBS Your bombs get more blast.

STICKY BOMB Throw timed sticky bombs.

"Choose Your Path" Upgrades

Path 1: Ignition
Fan the flames of your bombs

1,500 Gold	2,000 Gold

FLAMING BOMBS Ignite bombs with your Flame Breath.

FIRED UP! Flaming Bombs frazzle even more enemies.

Path 2: Reaction Satisfaction
Ring-a-ring of explosives!

1,500 Gold	2,000 Gold

RING OF FIRE Close the circle of fire to explode.

RING BLAST Rings of Fire spread wider.

Attack 2
Starting Power

ROCKET DASH Fire those rocket boots.

Power Upgrades

300 Gold	800 Gold	1,000 Gold

READY FOR BLAST OFF Charge your Rocket Dash to inflict more damage.

ARMOR PLATING Get a new suit of armor.

FUEL FOR THE FIRE Make your dash last longer.

"Choose Your Path" Upgrades

Path 1: Fuel-Injected
Get even more hot-footed

1,500 Gold	2,000 Gold

HEAT WAVE Rocket-fueled fireballs end each dash.

TEMPERED FIRE Heat Waves get hotter.

Path 2: Temperature's Rising
Give off a deadly glow!

1,500 Gold	2,000 Gold

FLAMED Dashes end with a fiery aura.

TOO HOT TO HANDLE Your aura gets more awesome.

FIRE KRAKEN

Fire Kraken singed anyone who threatened his home in the Blazing Ocean. When he was sure his tribe was safe, he turned to using his torch-like talents as a Skylander.

SOUL GEM
in Twisty Tunnels

DANCE OF DRAGONS Fire your dragon costume at unsuspecting enemies.

THE BIGGER ONE The biggest explosion imaginable.

STARTING STATS		PERSONALITY FILE
Max Health	260	Alert
Speed	43	Swift hunter
Armor	18	Spirited
Critical Hit	8	Bit of a show-off
Elemental Power	25	

SPECIAL QUEST

DON'T RAIN ON MY PARADE Hit 10 enemies with one parade attack.

Starting Power

Attack 1

SPARKLING STRIKES Swing your sparkling staff.

Power Upgrades

300 Gold

DRAGON PARADE Slip into a fiery dragon costume.

800 Gold

GLOW STICK Get yourself an impressive new staff.

1,000 Gold

RISING FOUNTAIN Charged staffs release explosions.

"Choose Your Path" Upgrades

Path 1: The Showcase
You just can get the staff these days!

1,500 Gold

RISING CHARGE Rising Fountains add explosions to next staff attacks.

2,000 Gold

FINALE! Rising Fountain affects a larger area.

Path 2: Magnificent Parade
Train your dragon attacks

1,500 Gold

YEAR OF THE DRAGON Dragon Parade lasts longer and does more damage.

2,000 Gold

DRAGON CANDLES Your dragon shoots fireworks at foes.

Starting Power

Attack 2

START THE SHOW! It's a firework attack. Ooooooh! Argggggh!

Power Upgrades

300 Gold

SHOW-OFF Three colorful projectiles are fired.

800 Gold

KRAKEN UP Jump up to deliver an explosive payload.

1,000 Gold

THE BIG ONE Light the fuse to a big explosion!

"Choose Your Path" Upgrades

Path 1: Stunning Sparkler
Put on an impressive firework display

1,500 Gold

UNSTABLE ELEMENT Near The Big One? Then you'll run faster.

2,000 Gold

SIZZLING SPARKLER Go into a spin with your staff.

Path 2: Booming Bouncer
Boost your fiery attacks

1,500 Gold

BIGBADABOOM Bounce attacks get more explosive.

2,000 Gold

STRIKE THE FOES The Big One knocks nearby enemies flying.

MEET THE SKYLANDERS

STAR STRIKE

"SHOOT FOR THE STARS!"

Accidently summoned to Skylands when Kaos sneezed during a spell, Star Strike soon joined the Skylanders and has been getting under evil's skin ever since.

SOUL GEM
in Rampant Ruins

SHOOTING STARS Shoot sparkly stars into nearby enemies.

STARTING STATS

Max Health	260
Speed	43
Armor	12
Critical Hit	8
Elemental Power	25

PERSONALITY FILE

Powerful
Mysterious
Wise
Discerning

SPECIAL QUEST

DEFLECTION MASTER Deflect return stars 20 times in a row.

Starting Powers

Attack 1

STAR GATE Summon an attacking star.

Attack 2

COSMIC TWIRL Go into a magical spin that reflects any nearby projectiles.

Power Upgrades

500 Gold

STARFALL Drop stars on your foes.

900 Gold

YOUR BIGGEST FAN Cosmic Twirls cover more distance.

700 Gold

STAR-FILLED SKY More shooting stars fall from above.

1,200 Gold

STAR POWER Shoot more impressive star shards at your enemies.

"Choose Your Path" Upgrades

Path 1: Star Gazer Get starry-eyed!

1,700 Gold

STAR LIGHT Starfall brings a colossal exploding star.

2,200 Gold

STAR STRUCK Super-duper stars splatter enemies.

3,000 Gold

STAR BRIGHT Starfall times two!

Path 2: Cosmic Reflector Ramp up your reflection abilities

1,700 Gold

ATOM SPLITTER Shoot starry projectiles at bad guys.

2,200 Gold

STAR EVASION That sparkling gown gets sturdier.

3,000 Gold

SUPER STAR Your star is rising–and growing, too!

DUNE BUG

"CAN'T BEAT THE BEETLE!"

Novice archivist Dune Bug sank the ancient Arkeyan library beneath the desert to protect its secrets from the marauding Sand Mages of Doom. Now he protects Skylands with his magical staff.

SOUL GEM
in Boney Islands

BUGGY BUDDY Summon a little friend to bug your enemies.

STARTING STATS		PERSONALITY FILE
Max Health	260	Protective
Speed	35	Quick-thinking
Armor	24	Pragmatic
Critical Hit	4	Well-read
Elemental Power	25	

SPECIAL QUEST

THAT'S HOW I ROLL Roll your Dune Ball 5,000 feet in all.

Starting Powers

Attack 1

MYSTIC MISSILES Zap magic beams from your staff.

Attack 2

DUNE BALL Sling a magic ball at anything that moves.

Power Upgrades

500 Gold

DUNE PARADE Increase the size of your Dune Ball, trapping enemies inside.

900 Gold

BURSTING MAGIC Get a new staff that fires rapid streams of magic.

700 Gold

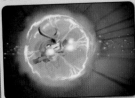

DEBILITATING DUNES Dune Balls cause more damage.

1,200 Gold

BUZZING BEETLE Take to the air with buzzing wings.

"Choose Your Path" Upgrades

Path 1: Scarab Sage Soup up your staff!

1,700 Gold

STUNNING SPREAD Charge up your staff to fire three magical orbs.

2,200 Gold

SCARAB POWER Get the Golden Staff for glittering magic blasts.

3,000 Gold

MAGIC SCARAB RIDE Jump while hovering to create magic shockwaves.

Path 2: Dune Mage Get some magical defenses

1,700 Gold

DUNE BOMB Dune Ball traps go bang!

2,200 Gold

HARDENED SHELL Get new super-tough (and stylish) armor.

3,000 Gold

SPARKING WINGS Sparks of pure magic stream out behind you.

PUNK SHOCK

"AMP IT UP!"

This undersea princess was happiest hunting to the sound of her beloved electro-music—until Snow Trolls put her kingdom on ice. Gill Grunt heard of her victory and suggested I recruit her as a Skylander.

SOUL GEM
in Kaos's Fortress

EELECTROCUTE Charge up your crossbow for an all-around onslaught.

STARTING STATS

Max Health	270
Speed	43
Armor	12
Critical Hit	8
Elemental Power	25

PERSONALITY FILE

Adventurous

Carefree

Born hunter

Avenging

SPECIAL QUEST

HYDROSTATICS Shock 100 enemies with Electrified Water Zones.

Attack 1

SPARK SHOT Fire electrified bolts. You can even zap water with them.

Attack 2

SPLASH BOMB Lob easily electrified water bombs.

Power Upgrades

500 Gold

SPARK SPLASH Zap enemies with your tail.

900 Gold

OHMG Spark Shots go three ways.

700 Gold

HIGH BOLTAGE Crossbolts cause more damage.

1,200 Gold

HYPERCHARGED Shock enemies with a speedy charge.

"Choose Your Path" Upgrades

Path 1: Conductor Construction Messing around with water!

1,700 Gold

H2THROW
Lob three water balls at once.

2,200 Gold

TROUBLED WATERS Water balloons bring more pain.

3,000 Gold

BOLTING BLOB Zap your water ball to electrify enemies near and far.

Path 2: Eel-ectrocutey Amp-up your electric attacks

1,700 Gold

Positively Charged Gain an electric glow that zaps nearby enemies.

2,200 Gold

IT HERTZ Electrified water delivers more juice.

3,000 Gold

RE-VOLTING SHOCK Tail-slap enemies into the air!

RIP TIDE

"GO FISH!"

Kaos got wind of the fact that I was taking an interest in this championship Aqua-Fighter and sent in his Squidface Brutes. Rip Tide soon battered them.

SOUL GEM
in Rampant Ruins

REINVENTING THE WHALE
Fighting fish burst from your whale's blowhole.

STARTING STATS		**PERSONALITY** FILE
Max Health	300	Competitive
Speed	43	Adaptable
Armor	30	No-nonsense
Critical Hit	4	Unrelenting
Elemental Power	25	

SPECIAL QUEST

WHALE OF A TIME Hurt 8 enemies at once with Whale On 'Em attacks.

Attack 1

TETRA ATTACK Swipe with either swordfish or shark.

Attack 2

FISH TOSS Fling your fish at foes.

Power Upgrades

500 Gold

WHALE ON 'EM Whack enemies with a whale. 'Nuff said.

900 Gold

FRESH FISH Throw a fish, and the next hit's a critical one.

700 Gold

BIGGER FISH TO FLY Increase the damage caused by your swordfish or shark.

1,200 Gold

BLISTERING BLUBBER Whales deliver more wallop.

"Choose Your Path" Upgrades

Path 1: Fishy Fencer Soup up your swordfish

1,700 Gold

NIPPING NEEDLE NOSE Fish-slapped enemies keep suffering.

2,200 Gold

PRACTICED PARRY Swordfish attack like never before.

3,000 Gold

STRAIGHT AS AN ANGLER Charge with your swordfish held high.

Path 2: Flounder Pounder Shark attacks get a boost

1,700 Gold

SHARK SURPRISE Hammer enemy heads with your hammerhead.

2,200 Gold

TIME TO HAMMER Hammerheads cause heavy damage from now on.

3,000 Gold

SHARK BITE BAIT Charge your shark to clear the path ahead.

COUNTDOWN

"I'M THE BOMB!"

  Every time Countdown explodes he loses a scrap of his memory. However, he never forgets to stand up to evil!

SOUL GEM
in Cascade Glade

SELF-DESTRUCT Blow a fuse that causes maximum damage.

STARTING STATS		PERSONALITY FILE
Max Health	290	Explosive
Speed	43	Forgetful
Armor	12	Impulsive
Critical Hit	8	Self-sacrificing
Elemental Power	25	

SPECIAL QUEST

OUT WITH A BANG Defeat 10 enemies at once by self-destructing.

Starting Powers

Attack 1

ROCKET BLAST Fire an angry rocket at foes.

Attack 2

BOMB HEAD Shoot your own head at enemies. Extreme!

Power Upgrades

500 Gold

CONTROLLED BURST Charge up and fire an even larger rocket.

900 Gold

EXPLOSIVE FRIENDSHIP Summon a bomb buddy to your side.

700 Gold

ROARING ROCKETS Rockets do more damage. It's a blast.

1,200 Gold

HEFTY CONCUSSION Get a bigger bomb head!

"Choose Your Path" Upgrades

Path 1: Boom Buddies Forever Get an explosive combination

1,700 Gold

BOOM BUDDIES Have four bomb pals at once.

2,200 Gold

BOMBING BLITZERS Your cute little bombs cause more damage. Aww!

3,000 Gold

LINGERING SPARKS Bomb buddies spark flames from their fuses.

Path 2: Rocketeer Get mega-missiles!

1,700 Gold

TRIPLE THREAT In case one missile isn't enough, have two more!

2,200 Gold

WARHEAD HANDS Every single rocket attack does more damage.

3,000 Gold

MEGA MORTAR Controlled Bursts inflict damage over a wider area. Boom!

WIND-UP

"ALL WOUND UP!"

Created by a time-obsessed toymaker, Wind-Up defended the temporal toy shop from chrono-crazed cyclopses. He would go on to become a timely member of the Skylanders.

SOUL GEM
in Iron Jaw Gulch

SPRING-LOADED CRANK
Automatically wind up during faster runs.

STARTING STATS		PERSONALITY FILE
Max Health	250	Punctual
Speed	43	Reliable
Armor	12	Bursting with energy
Critical Hit	4	Master strategist
Elemental Power	25	

SPECIAL QUEST
ALL WOUND UP Cause damage of 2,500 when overcranked.

Attack 1

SHORT CIRCUIT Sparking claws attack nearby enemies.

Attack 2

WIND UP! Wind yourself into an enemy-beating spin.

Power Upgrades

500 Gold

OVERCRANK STABILIZER Overcrank your wind-up meter for a big bang.

900 Gold

SPRING SHOT Boing! Spring shots fire enemies into orbit.

700 Gold

WINDING WEAPON Enemies get wound up, too!

1,200 Gold

POWER PISTONS Give yourself more punch.

"Choose Your Path" Upgrades

Path 1: Toy Box It's child's play!

1,700 Gold

CYMBALS Slam enemies with your shiny cymbals.

2,200 Gold

CRASH CYMBALS Louder crashes mean more damage.

3,000 Gold

TOY GUN Fire sink plungers at those baddies.

Path 2: Winder Become a wind-up artist!

1,700 Gold

WINDUP PUNCH Get a MASSIVE boxing glove!

2,200 Gold

AUTO WINDUP Taking damage automatically adds to your windup.

3,000 Gold

POWER CRANK Overcranking pulls enemies in.

ZOO LOU

"NATURE CALLS!"

It was Double Trouble who brought this steadfast shaman to my attention, after Zoo Lou freed his tribe from invading trolls.

SOUL GEM
in Mudwater Hollow

BIRDS OF PREY Summon up to five feathered friends.

STARTING STATS

Max Health	290
Speed	43
Armor	18
Critical Hit	6
Elemental Power	25

PERSONALITY FILE

Inquisitive

Has a warrior's heart

At one with nature

Passionate

SPECIAL QUEST

PROFESSIONAL BOAR RIDER Hit an enemy during 20 full-length boar rides.

Attack 1

BIRD CALL Birds swoop in on nearby enemies.

Attack 2

WOLF CALL A canine companion wolfs down foes.

Power Upgrades

500 Gold

PIGGYBACK RIDE Ride on the back of a wild boar.

700 Gold

RAGING BOAR Your piggy pal gets a power-up.

900 Gold

SWOOP RE-LOOP Spirit birds target enemies twice before flying away.

1,200 Gold

BETTER BEAKS Those birdies just got badder!

"Choose Your Path" Upgrades

Path 1: The Bucking Boar Boost your boar action

1,700 Gold

ROUGH RIDER Boar-riding throws rocks and dust at enemies.

2,200 Gold

THICKER PIGSKIN Get an even thicker hide.

3,000 Gold

HOG WILD Your boar continues its barrage after you've jumped off.

Path 2: The Wild Wolf The pack is back!

1,700 Gold

ALPHA WOLF Summon stronger wolves.

2,200 Gold

HUNGER OF THE WOLF Wolf attacks bring increased speed.

3,000 Gold

HUNTER AND GATHERER Your wolf finds you food when you need it.

BUMBLE BLAST

"THE PERFECT SWARM!"

Powered by magic honey, this living beehive offered his services as a defender of nature. "Sweet," as I believe they say in your world.

SOUL GEM
in Mudwater Hollow

BEE-PACK BACKPACK Your backpack automatically fires bees at bad guys.

STARTING STATS		PERSONALITY FILE
Max Health	320	Natural guardian
Speed	35	Valiant
Armor	24	Fearless
Critical Hit	4	Sticks with his friends
Elemental Power	25	

SPECIAL QUEST

NOT THE BEES! Hit honey-coated enemies with bees 125 times.

Attack 1

BEEZOOKA Shoot homing honey bees at enemies.

Attack 2

HONEY GLOB Cover enemies in yummy honey.

Power Upgrades

500 Gold

HONEY BEECON Bees make a beeline for enemies covered in honey.

900 Gold

HIVE MIND Leave beehive minds ready to blow.

700 Gold

HUNGRY BEES Bees deliver increased damage to honey-covered foes.

1,200 Gold

PAINFUL STINGS Bees get souped-up stingers.

"Choose Your Path" Upgrades

Path 1: Bee Keeper Boost your bumblebees

1,700 Gold

BEE ARMADA Get a swarm of three bees.

2,200 Gold

STIRRED UP A NEST Your new beezooka causes a buzz.

3,000 Gold

QUEEN BEE Deliver them a royal pain in the butt.

Path 2: Honey Tree It's a sticky end for your enemies

1,700 Gold

HONEY BUZZ BLAST Your honey already contains bees!

2,200 Gold

HEAVY HONEY Honey attacks get a buzzing boost.

3,000 Gold

HONEYCOMB BARK Get tougher—and stickier—armor.

GRIM CREEPER

"YOUR TIME IS UP!"

One of the finest reapers ever to wield a scythe, Grim Creeper sends spooks screaming. Followers of the Darkness aren't too fond of him, either.

SOUL GEM
in Iron Jaw Gulch

HELP FROM BEYOND A ghost manifests from defeated enemies to protect you.

STARTING STATS		PERSONALITY FILE
Max Health	250	Brave
Speed	43	Daring
Armor	6	Determined
Critical Hit	8	Unyielding
Elemental Power	25	

SPECIAL QUEST

AGGRESSIVE OUTFIT Hit 10 enemies in a row with your armor when it returns to you.

Attack 1

SCYTHE SWING Swipe your spooky scythe at your enemies.

Attack 2

GHOST FORM Slip out of your armor to attack in spectral form, while your armor continues the fight.

Power Upgrades

500 Gold

POLTERGEIST SCYTHE Your scythe spins off on its own.

700 Gold

SPIRIT SCYTHE Scythes spin with more force.

900 Gold

SPOOK AND DESTROY Touch enemies in ghost form for your armor to target them.

1,200 Gold

ARMORED AMORE Animated armor does more damage as it flies back to you.

"Choose Your Path" Upgrades

Path 1: Grim Scythe Style The grimmest creeper gets grimmer

1,700 Gold

SPHERE OF FEAR Scythe spins in a larger arc.

2,200 Gold

GRAVE DANGER Increase your Critical Hits.

3,000 Gold

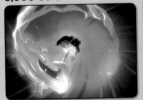

GHASTLY DAMAGE Enemies hit by the living armor take more damage.

Path 2: Spooky Specter Liven up your living armor

1,700 Gold

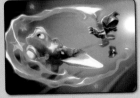

IT'S ALIVE! Living armor fights back when attacked.

2,200 Gold

HAUNTED HELP Enemies between your ghost form and living armor feel the pain.

3,000 Gold

SOUL SAMPLER Gain health for every enemy you hit using Spook and Destroy.

ROLLER BRAWL

"LET'S ROLL!"

Roller Brawl joined the Skylanders after Kaos kidnapped her five older brothers—and all because he was in love with the impressive vampire jammer! She still makes him fall head-over-heels, but only when she attacks!

SOUL GEM
in Iron Jaw Gulch

CURSED HELMET Create a link between helmet and enemy, spelling bad news for nearby baddies.

STARTING STATS		PERSONALITY FILE
Max Health	260	Speedy
Speed	50	Cunning
Armor	12	Single-minded
Critical Hit	8	Resourceful
Elemental Power	25	

SPECIAL QUEST
SHARP JAMMER Defeat 10 enemies at once using Deadly Clothesline.

Attack 1

ROLLER CLAWS Swipe your claws at any enemies near you.

Attack 2

DERBY DASH Dash ahead, damaging nearby foes.

Power Upgrades

500 Gold

SKATEBLADES Fire ice-skate blades at enemies.

900 Gold

DEADLY CLOTHESLINE Rush again, clotheslining anyone in your way.

700 Gold

IMPACT SKATER Dash attacks cause more damage.

1,200 Gold

AGGRESSION Fangs for these even sharper claws.

"Choose Your Path" Upgrades

Path 1: Shadow Skater Vamp up your skating skills

1,700 Gold

PIROUETTE Skate in a vicious circle, slicing at nearby enemies.

2,200 Gold

HARDENED HELM Slip on a new helmet for extra protection.

3,000 Gold

BULLRUSH Rush at enemies, knocking them away.

Path 2: Skateblade Siren Take those blades for a spin

1,700 Gold

SKATEBLADE TRAP Spring a trap on the opposition.

2,200 Gold

CRITICAL CLAWS The stakes are raised as your claws sharpen.

3,000 Gold

SPINNING SAWS She spins sharp saws to make her enemies sore.

SLOBBER TOOTH

"CLOBBER AND SLOBBER!"

Kaos once tried to launch an attack on Slobber Tooth's brothers and sisters while they were hibernating. Big mistake! The evil Portal Master was slobbered into next week!

SOUL GEM
in Cascade Glade

IRON JAW Head attacks chew up the opposition with an iron bite.

STARTING STATS

Max Health	300
Speed	35
Armor	30
Critical Hit	2
Elemental Power	25

PERSONALITY FILE

Gruff
Stubborn
Willful
Deep sleeper

SPECIAL QUEST

HUNGRY LIKE A HIPPO Gobble up 25 enemies.

Starting Powers

Attack 1

HORN SWIPE Butt bad guys when they least expect it.

Attack 2

CHOMP & CHUCK Chew 'em up and spit 'em out.

Power Upgrades

500 Gold

UNSTOPPABLE FORCE Barrel forward in a butting frenzy.

900 Gold

SHOCKWAVE It's slamming time!

700 Gold

TOUGH HIDE Have yourself some more armor-as if you need it.

1,200 Gold

LOOGEY Spit enemies over a greater distance.

"Choose Your Path" Upgrades

Path 1: Food Fighter Eat yourself to victory!

1,700 Gold

SNOT ROCKET Cover enemies in boogers.

2,200 Gold

OM NOM NOM Chomped enemies help to feed you a healthy diet.

3,000 Gold

FEAST Inhale foes into your massive mouth.

Path 2: Seismic Tail Tail attacks cause tremors

1,700 Gold

FLING Tail slams fling enemies into the air.

2,200 Gold

WEIGHT GAIN Your tail gains some stony spikes.

3,000 Gold

EARTH SHAKER Add a twist to your tail with shocking rocks.

SCORP

"KING OF THE STING!"

The former Sting Ball champion realized that there was more to life than sports when he rescued his spectators from a magical flood. Now he fights for all of Skylands.

SOUL GEM
in Motleyville

AVALANCHE DASH Curl up into a ball and crush!

STARTING STATS		**PERSONALITY** FILE
Max Health	260	Agile
Speed	35	Fearless
Armor	18	Gritty
Critical Hit	8	Bold
Elemental Power	25	

SPECIAL QUEST

TICKING SLIME BOMB 50 enemies must fall foul of your poison.

Starting Powers

Attack 1

EMERALD CRYSTAL Chuck gloopy explosive gems.

Attack 2

TAIL STING Poison enemies with a flick of your tail.

Power Upgrades

500 Gold

BOULDER ROLL A rolling stone splatters more enemies.

900 Gold

CRYSTAL BALL Two sticky crystals become one.

700 Gold

CHROME CARAPACE Get shiny new plate armor.

1,200 Gold

EARTHLY POWER Explosive crystals cause more damage.

"Choose Your Path" Upgrades

Path 1: Stinger Titanic tail attacks ahoy!

1,700 Gold

FUMING FISSURE Create shockwaves with a super stinger slam.

2,200 Gold

SCORPION STRIKE Tail goes off the scale.

3,000 Gold

POTENT POISONS Enemies struggle to shake off poison strikes.

Path 2: Crystal Venomancer Charge up your crystals!

1,700 Gold

CRACKED CRYSTALS Gloopy crystals damage a greater area.

2,200 Gold

CRYSTAL SHARDS It's crystal clear why these shattering spheres cause so much damage.

3,000 Gold

VENOMOUS CRYSTALS Crystals split into perfect poisonous pairs.

SCRATCH

"THE LUCK OF THE CLAW!"

Sassy Scratch was recruited by Jet-Vac after she saved the Cat's Eye Mountain from Pirate Greebles.

SOUL GEM
in Fantasm Forest

GEM AFFINITY Collect coins, gold, and gems to gain health.

STARTING STATS

Max Health	260
Speed	50
Armor	6
Critical Hit	8
Elemental Power	25

PERSONALITY FILE

Curious
Creative
Plucky
Playful

SPECIAL QUEST

PURRFECT POUNCE Pounce on—and defeat—50 enemies.

Attack 1

CAT SCRATCH Turn enemies into scratching posts.

Attack 2

PLAYFUL POUNCE Leap onto a laser pointer.

Power Upgrades

500 Gold

WING SPARK Dodge attacks, flicking enemies away.

900 Gold

WHIRLWING Suck foes into an energy-sapping spin.

700 Gold

SILVER CLAWS Spring a new pair of silvery claws.

1,200 Gold

SILVER MASK Mask laser takes the shine off enemies.

"Choose Your Path" Upgrades

Path 1: Ruby Red for danger!

1,700 Gold

SHARPENED RUBIES Cat's eyes blaze brighter than ever.

2,200 Gold

RUBY RAGE Charge those claws to cut deeper.

3,000 Gold

RUBY MASK Laser blasts spread out wider.

Path 2: Sapphire Deliver a bolt from the blue!

1,700 Gold

SPEEDY SAPPHIRE The fastest feline you will ever see.

2,200 Gold

SAPPHIRE SLASH Whip up a vortex with your wings.

3,000 Gold

SAPPHIRE MASK Laser attacks slow enemies caught in your gaze.

POP THORN

"STRAIGHT TO THE POINT!"

For centuries, the timid Pufferthorns were used as combs by giant hairy trolls—until Pop Thorn bravely stood up for his cute cousins.

SOUL GEM
in Mount Cloudbreak

TO PUFF OR NOT TO PUFF
Pop to increase speed. Puff to increase armor. The choice is yours.

STARTING STATS		**PERSONALITY** FILE
Max Health	280	Cheerful
Speed	43	No pushover
Armor	24	Fighter for justice
Critical Hit	6	Unique
Elemental Power	25	

SPECIAL QUEST
TAKE A DEEP BREATH Hit enemies with a single breath 100 times in a row.

Attack 1

PUFF Puff out to shoot poisoned spines.

Attack 2

POP Deflate to deliver a deadly gust.

Power Upgrades

500 Gold

FRESH BREATH Gusts get more powerful.

900 Gold

POLISHED SPIKES It's sharper spine time.

700 Gold

PUFFBALL POUND Puffing up sends out shockwaves.

1,200 Gold

WIND TRAP Spine mines pop into existence.

"Choose Your Path" Upgrades

Path 1: Tough and Puffed Well, that's just swell

1,700 Gold

ROLLERPUFF Rough up enemies with a puffed-up roll.

2,200 Gold

BOUNCEBACK Puff projectiles out of the way.

3,000 Gold

PRICKLY BODY Getting attacked unleashes a prickly problem.

Path 2: Controlled Breather Boost your breathing techniques

1,700 Gold

AERO TRAMPOLINE Bounce your way out of a puff.

2,200 Gold

DEEP BREATH Three times the puff.

3,000 Gold

SCATTERED WINDS Breathe out multiple air projectiles.

FRYNO

"CRASH AND BURN!"

Fryno turned his back on the Blazing Biker Brigade when he discovered they were nothing more than a bunch of crooks.

SOUL GEM
in Frostfest Mountains

MADNESS MAXED Add fuel to Fryno's fiery temper.

STARTING STATS		**PERSONALITY** FILE
Max Health	300	Honest
Speed	43	Furious
Armor	6	Bullish
Critical Hit	4	A fighter
Elemental Power	25	

SPECIAL QUEST

FREQUENT FRIER Frazzle 100 enemies with red-hot attacks.

Attack 1

BRAWL The hotter you get, the harder you punch.

Attack 2

HEATED Turn up the heat by thumping the ground.

Power Upgrades

500 Gold

THE HORN AND THE HOG Charge forward with extra wheeled action when angry.

900 Gold

FIRED UP! Throw a titanic temper tantrum.

700 Gold

BUILT TOUGH Need a boost? Have some health.

1,200 Gold

MOLTEN FURY Anger fuels awesome attacks.

"Choose Your Path" Upgrades

Path 1: Brawler Get fists of fury!

1,700 Gold

HOT HANDS Rapidly punch enemies to release heat.

2,200 Gold

SPIKED UP Add heavy-metal to your heavy hitters.

3,000 Gold

TEMPERATURE TANTRUM Nearby enemies get hot under the collar.

Path 2: Fryno's Hot Shop Burn up the road!

1,700 Gold

BORN TO RIDE Blazing bikes are yours with every Horn and Hog.

2,200 Gold

HOT ROD Motorbike attacks get maxed out.

3,000 Gold

CRASH AND BURN Bike rides end with a bang.

SMOLDERDASH

"A BLAZE OF GLORY!"

  After saving the sacred First Flame from Kaos (he was using it to light his birthday candles), Smolderdash was offered a place in the royal defense force. She declined, as she wanted to become a Skylander.

SOUL GEM
in Woodburrow

SMOLDER DASH Cover your eyes—it's an extreme eclipse!

STARTING STATS

Max Health	280	
Speed	43	
Armor	12	
Critical Hit	8	
Elemental Power	25	

PERSONALITY FILE

Ambitious
Swift
Fierce
Illuminating

SPECIAL QUEST

EVENT HORIZON Singe 50 enemies with a single supernova.

Attack 1

FLAME WHIP Whip enemies into shape.

Attack 2

SOLAR ORB A ball of pure solar activity—ready to blow.

Power Upgrades

500 Gold

ECLIPSE Shine like the sun for stronger attacks.

900 Gold

SUNRISE Slam a small sun into Skylands.

700 Gold

SOLAR-POWERED Travel at the speed of light.

1,200 Gold

WHIP IT! Your whip gets lashings of solar power.

'Choose Your Path' Upgrades

Path 1: Sun Forger Become a solar star!

1,700 Gold

SUPER GIANT Supersize those Solar Orbs.

2,200 Gold

SOLAR FLARE Your Critical Hit flares up.

3,000 Gold

SUN SPLITTER Slice one sun into two with a crack of your whip.

Path 2: Sun-Forged Let there be light!

1,700 Gold

SOLAR BLAST Five small suns burst out of every sunrise.

2,200 Gold

SUNNY ARMOR Become a knight in shining armor.

3,000 Gold

SUN'S CORE Throw entire suns at enemies or gain a blazing halo.

Your Skylander

Of course, it is not just my new Skylanders that can aid your quest. These faithful champions from days gone by are also ready and willing to jump into battle . . .

FIRE
Lava Barf Eruptor
Fire Bone Hot Dog

UNDEAD
Phantom Cynder
Twin Blade Chop Chop

LIFE
Thorn Horn Camo
Ninja Stealth Elf

AIR
Horn Blast Whirlwind
Turbo Jet-Vac
Lightcore Warnado

Collection

MAGIC
Super Gulp Pop Fizz
Mega Ram Spyro

WATER
Anchors Away Gill Grunt
Blizzard Chill
Lightcore Wham-Shell

TECH
Big Bang Trigger Happy
Heavy Duty Sprocket

EARTH
Knockout Terrafin
Lightcore Flashwing
Hyper Beam Prism Break

SWAP Challenges

Each SWAP Force Skylander comes with a unique SWAP ability, completely separate from their Element. They can use this to access special SWAP Zones scattered throughout the Cloudbreak Islands. Each one presents a very different challenge.

TYPES OF SWAP ZONE

SPIN

Go into a spin to destroy the barriers between you and the statue of Kaos.

HINT: Be careful around the edges of the platforms. Hit the block too many times and you won't be able to stop yourself from spinning over the side. Fatal!

CLIMB

Clamber up vertical walls, avoiding hazards from above. Time your wall dashes right and you can sprint ahead.

HINT: Use the barriers for shelter when you need it most.

SNEAK

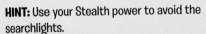

Time to get sneaky. Creep around enemy bases to locate the power supply— then blow the place sky high!

HINT: Use your Stealth power to avoid the searchlights.

BOUNCE

Leap from platform to platform to burst the balloons with Kaos's ugly face on them. Warning: Some platforms crumble away to dust.

HINT: Use your Bounce power for an extra boost between platforms.

DIG

Head below the ground to find three blue gems. Avoid mine carts as you race against the clock.

HINT: You'll be in the dark, so don't worry if it takes you more than one attempt to locate all three jewels.

ROCKET

Race your way through the rings, avoiding floating objects and trying to beat the clock.

HINT: Every time you make it through a ring, you'll earn back valuable seconds.

SPEED

It's another time trial. Use your turbo boost to race to the finish line. Simple.

HINT: Don't crash into any obstacles. They'll only slow you down.

TELEPORT

These are tricky challenges. Teleport from platform to platform to gather three magical runes.

HINT: Keep an eye on the glowing halos. They mean the platforms are about to vanish beneath your feet.

SWAP ABILITY	SWAP-ZONE LOCATION	CHALLENGE UNLOCKED
Bounce	Cascade Glade	Sunny Heights
Bounce	Frostfest Mountains	Frosty Frolicking
Bounce	Kaos's Fortress	Kaotic Spring
Bounce	Rampant Ruins	Lonely Springs
Bounce	Twisty Tunnels	Parched Heights
Climb	Boney Island	Amber Ice Climb
Climb	Kaos's Fortress	Tower of Falling Goo
Climb	Motleyville	Junkside Climb
Climb	Mount Cloudbreak	Tree Top Jaunt
Climb	Rampant Ruins	Robot Ramparts
Climb	Tower of Time	Windy Tower
Dig	Boney Island	Ice Hollows
Dig	Frostfest Mountains	Glacial Descent
Dig	Iron Jaw Gulch	Submerged Sands
Dig	Mount Cloudbreak	Spiky Pit
Dig	Tower of Time	Tick-Tock Tunneling
Rocket	Boney Island	Ice Cold Flying
Rocket	Cascade Glade	Woodlands Speedstacle
Rocket	Iron Jaw Gulch	Storm of Sands
Rocket	Sheep Wreck Islands	Sheep Strafing
Rocket	Fantasm Forest	Fire Flighter
Rocket	Mount Cloudbreak	Forest Flyby
Rocket	Mudwater Hollow	Tree Scraping
Sneak	Cascade Glade	Area Fifty Tree
Sneak	Fantasm Forest	Fire Fortress
Sneak	Frostfest Mountains	Nerves of Ice
Sneak	Twisty Tunnels	Sunken Sand Base
Sneak	Sheep Wreck Islands	Wool Over Their Eyes
Speed	Kaos's Fortress	Greenlight Raceway
Speed	Motleyville	Drag Stripped
Speed	Rampant Ruins	Frenetic Fog
Speed	Winter Keep	Wind Whipped
Spin	Motleyville	Twisted Towers
Spin	Mudwater Hollow	Marbled Gardens
Spin	Tower of Time	Spinning Cogs
Spin	Twisty Tunnels	Warped Sands
Spin	Winter Keep	Frozen Top
Teleport	Fantasm Forest	Ethereal Transfer
Teleport	Iron Jaw Gulch	Hourglass Blink
Teleport	Mudwater Hollow	Going Whoosh
Teleport	Winter Keep	Flash Frost
Teleport	Sheep Wreck Islands	Beached Blinkout

EON'S TIP
Collect as many Winged Rubies in the challenges as possible for extra riches.

THE FORCES OF DARKNESS

KAOS

"EVIL PORTAL MASTER AND ALL-AROUND BAD GUY"

 Say what you want about my odious archenemy, but he's certainly persistent. No matter how many times he's been defeated by the Skylanders, Kaos bounces back to unleash more, well, chaos.

Much of Kaos's early life remains a mystery. We know he was born into a particularly evil royal family, but we don't know why they kicked him out at the earliest opportunity.

Of course, Kaos himself claims that he left of his own accord, in order to conquer all of Skylands, but this could easily be a lie. There's a possibility he set out on his own to prove himself to his dismissive (and thoroughly despicable) mother, who quickly decided her diminutive son was an utter waste of space.

Perhaps this is why he lost all of his hair. No one can tell—but Skylands is populated by many bizarre and twisted creations summoned by Kaos in his quest to invent the perfect anti-baldness potion.

PERSONALITY FILE

Megalomaniacal
Self-centered to
 the extreme
Completely and utterly
 evil

GLUMSHANKS

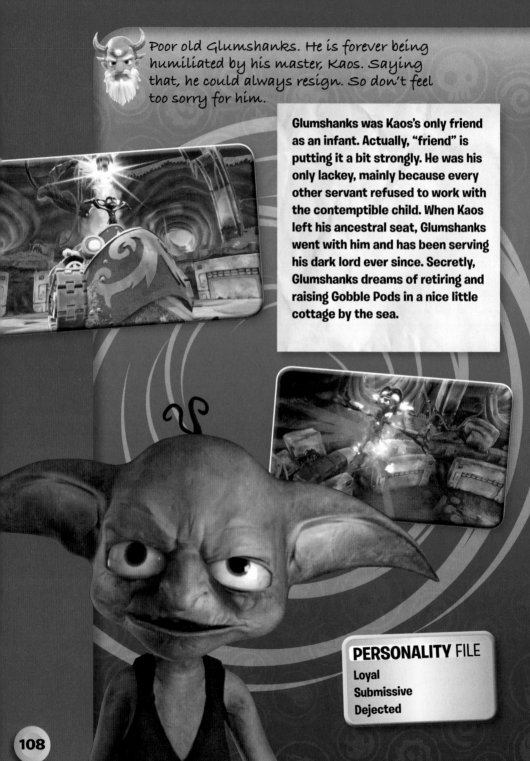

Poor old Glumshanks. He is forever being humiliated by his master, Kaos. Saying that, he could always resign. So don't feel too sorry for him.

Glumshanks was Kaos's only friend as an infant. Actually, "friend" is putting it a bit strongly. He was his only lackey, mainly because every other servant refused to work with the contemptible child. When Kaos left his ancestral seat, Glumshanks went with him and has been serving his dark lord ever since. Secretly, Glumshanks dreams of retiring and raising Gobble Pods in a nice little cottage by the sea.

PERSONALITY FILE
Loyal
Submissive
Dejected

KAOS'S MOM

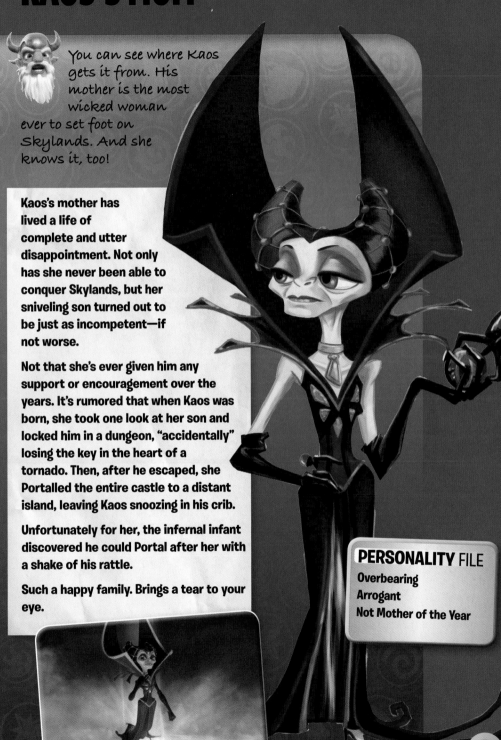

You can see where Kaos gets it from. His mother is the most wicked woman ever to set foot on Skylands. And she knows it, too!

Kaos's mother has lived a life of complete and utter disappointment. Not only has she never been able to conquer Skylands, but her sniveling son turned out to be just as incompetent—if not worse.

Not that she's ever given him any support or encouragement over the years. It's rumored that when Kaos was born, she took one look at her son and locked him in a dungeon, "accidentally" losing the key in the heart of a tornado. Then, after he escaped, she Portalled the entire castle to a distant island, leaving Kaos snoozing in his crib.

Unfortunately for her, the infernal infant discovered he could Portal after her with a shake of his rattle.

Such a happy family. Brings a tear to your eye.

PERSONALITY FILE
Overbearing
Arrogant
Not Mother of the Year

KNOW YOUR ENEMY

Beware, Portal Master. Skylands may be full of wonder, but it is also teeming with hideous horrors, foul freaks, and vile villains. Study these pages carefully. Your Skylanders' lives may depend on it!

Air Spell Punk

First seen in Twisty Tunnels

Makes your enemies light on their feet.

Air Geargolem

First seen in Twisty Tunnels

A golem determined to put you into a spin.

Arkeyan Barrelbot

First seen in Rampant Ruins

This spook-tacular robot packs quite a shock. Avoid that ectoplasmic energy.

Arkeyan Knuckleduster

First seen in Jungle Rumble

This bot-brawler certainly punches above its weight.

Arkeyan Rip-Rotor

First seen in Rampant Ruins

Spinning blades that can zap you from above. Hit 'em when they touch down.

Arkeyan Slamshock

First seen in Rampant Ruins

This venerable bot is vulnerable just after it's discharged.

Baron Von Shellshock

First seen in Motleyville

This crooked crab loves order even though he works for Kaos. The hook-clawed crustacean is also fond of building scuttling war-machines out of scrap!

DID YOU KNOW?

It was Baron Von Shellshock who discovered Kaos's haul of petrified Darkness. The evil Portal Master promised him a town to rule once Skylands had fallen. Just a town? It's fair to say that the baron isn't the most ambitious of crabs.

Boom Boss

First seen in Twisty Tunnels

Forget about throwing bombs. This troll chucks entire crates of explosives.

EON'S TIP

Tackle Boom Bosses when they're reloading.

Bubba Greeb

First seen in Motherly Mayhem

Bubba Greeb is Kaos's Mom's pride and joy. She's had him ever since he was a pup. Despite his size, he's not much of a brawler—he'd rather throw smaller minions at his foes. The big coward.

Cadet Crusher

First seen in Twisty Tunnels

If he had a hammer, he'd try to smash you in the face . . . oh look, he does!

Chompy

First seen in Mount Cloudbreak

Small and nippy, this ghastly green glutton will eat anything it meets.

Chompy Blitzbloom

First seen in Winter Keep

Look out below! Chompies from heaven!

Chompy Boomblossom

First seen in Fantasm Forest

A Chompy that explodes? What will they think of next?

Chompy Frostflower

First seen in Boney Islands

This Chompy's bite will leave you cold.

Chompy Pastepetal

First seen in Kaos's Fortress

Splits into two smaller Chompy Cyclopses.

Chompy Pod

First seen in Mount Cloudbreak

Pesky plant that spawns Chompies. Destroy it to stop the flood of little green ankle-biters.

DID YOU KNOW?

A Chompy Pod's color reflects the color of the Chompies it spawns.

Chompy Powerhouse

First seen in Motleyville

Cybernetic Chompy with even more bite.

Chompy Rustbud

First seen in Rampant Ruins

Undead robo-biter from beyond the grave.

Clock Geargolem

First seen in Tower of Time

This spinning golem can only clock off if you freeze time.

Cyclops Sleetthrower

First seen in Winter Keep

Look! That cyclops is clearing the path. How helpful. Oh wait, it's throwing the snow at you. Not so helpful after all.

Coldspear Cyclops

First seen in Boney Islands

What an eyeful! This mono-orbed minion lives to jab and poke!

Cyclops Snowblaster

First seen in Boney Islands

This is no gentle game of snowballs. There's nothing nice about the blaster's ice missiles.

Cyclops Brawlbuckler

First seen in Frostfest Mountains

Knock out its shield first—then finish it off!

Earth Geargolem

First seen in Motleyville

Jump over this giant's shockwaves to survive a fight.

Cyclops Gazermage

First seen in Boney Islands

Magical eye beams get magnified through the looking glass.

Evilized Boghog

First seen in Mudwater Hollow

The Boghog is a passive, gentle creature—until it gets Evilized! Remove the crystals to de-Evilize.

Evilized Greeble

First seen in Cascade Glade

Bad enough before it's been blasted by Kaos's Evilizer, this dark purple Greeble is far more difficult to deal with. Watch out for those swords.

Evilized Chillydog

First seen in Frostfest Mountain

Throws fiery snowballs. I'm not sure if that's cool or not.

Evilized Sugarbat

First seen in Rampant Ruins

Once Evilized, this fearsome fanged fiend will try to dive-bomb you from up high.

Evil Glumshanks

First seen in Jungle Rumble

Kaos's right-hand troll can move missiles through the power of his Evilized mind. Who knew?

Evilized Whiskers

First seen in Motleyville

Oh no! Tessa's best bird has gone bad! Release it by smashing the crystals when it gets its head stuck in the ground.

Evilized Kangarat

First seen in Iron Jaw Gulch

This bouncing baddy will try to get the jump on you with its gem-encrusted tail.

Evilized Screecher

First seen in Fantasm Forest

Don't be a twit-twoo. It's wise to dodge this bird's wicked wingspan.

Evilized Snowroller

First seen in Iron Jaw Gulch

Wait until this cool customer rolls into a warrior, then destroy its crystals while it's stunned.

Fire Geargolem

First seen in Iron Jaw Gulch

This hunk of burning gears will throw a little heat your way.

Gobble Pod

First seen in Cascade Glade

Hang on! This is in the wrong section. The Gobble Pod only eats enemies. What a helpful plant. Or animal. Or whatever it is . . .

Greeble

First seen in Mount Cloudbreak

Not the brightest minion in Kaos's army, the Greeble should pose no real threat to a Skylander.

Greeble Blunderbuss

First seen in Cascade Glade

Evilized screwball with even more firepower.

Greeble Heaver

First seen in Motleyville

This Greeble's gun delivers not one but three blasts.

Greeble Ironclad

First seen in Cascade Glade

Wait until the tea-loving armored juggernaut drops its guard—then attack!

Greeble Screwballs

First seen in Mount Cloudbreak

A Greeble with a bazooka almost as big as it is. I think the gun is slightly more intelligent, to be honest.

Grumblebum Rocketshooter

First seen in Mudwater Hollow

Only a Greeble would build a gun turret from a tree. Those rockets are nasty, though.

Grumblebum Trasher

First seen in Mudwater Hollow

Three eyes, one club—and a tendency to overbalance!

Ice Geargolem

First seen in Winter Keep

Its icicle missiles will cold snap you in two.

K-Bot Gloopgunner

First seen in Kaos's Fortress

Shoots globules of detonating goo!

K-Bot Mineminer

First seen in Kaos's Fortress

This bomb-lobbing bot will teleport before it's destroyed.

K-Bot Splodeshard

First seen in Kaos's Fortress

Always ready to splat you with its spinning shards.

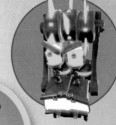

EON'S TIP

Get the Grumblebum while it's reloading!

Life Spell Punk

First seen in Mudwater Hollow

This meddlesome mage will restore an enemy's health, so always go after it first.

Loose Cannon

First seen in Boney Island

Wooden armor? You've got to be joking. Although there's nothing funny about that steam-powered cannon!

Magic Spell Punk

First seen in Kaos's Fortress

Can make enemies invisible with a single spell.

Mesmeralda

First seen in Frostfest Mountains

This showstopping spider has a cast of deadly puppets waiting in the wings. Exploding snowmen and spinning dancers? The stage is set for a blockbuster battle.

EON'S TIP

Missile Maulers can often be found hiding in crates.

Missile Mauler

First seen in Fantasm Forest

Watch it! This troll's missiles never fly straight.

Mr. Chompy

First seen in Kaos's Fortress

There's nothing unusual about this Chompy. Oh, other than the fact he's huge, of course—and duplicates when you attack. Actually, that is quite unusual, isn't it?

Pirate Powderkeg

First seen in Iron Jaw Gulch

A buccaneer Greeble with a great big blunderbuss.

Pirate Slamspin

First seen in Iron Jaw Gulch

Wait for this spinning swashbuckler to get dizzy.

Tech Geargolem

First seen in Fantasm Forest

It's got guns up its sleeves. In fact, they are its sleeves.

Time Spell Punk

First seen in Tower of Time

Unfreezes time at the most inconvenient moment.

Twistpick Cyclops

First seen in Winter Keep

Hit it before it starts pinwheeling those petrifying picks.

Undead Spell Punk

First seen in Fantasm Forest

Able to raise the dead, which is just plain rude really. Take it out before it unleashes a horde of skeletal trolls.

DID YOU KNOW?

Some Spell Punks can magically disguise themselves as just about anything else. In fact, for all I know you might be a Spell Punk. You're not, are you?

INTO THE ADVENTURE

CHAPTER 1

MOUNT CLOUDBREAK

Tessa has interrupted Flynn's vacation with a plea for help. He's never been able to resist a pretty face—or trouble. With the *Dread-Yacht* under attack there's only one way to go— into the fiery depths of the volcano itself!

Goal
○ Get to Woodburrow

Dares
○ Find Flynn's missing stuff
○ Defeat 50 enemies
○ Get through with no Skylanders defeated

Items
○ 3 Treasure Chests
○ 2 Soul Gems
○ 1 Legendary Treasure
○ 3 Hats
○ 1 Bonus Mission Map
○ 1 Story Scroll
○ 1 Giant Treasure Chest
○ 1 Winged Sapphire

Areas
○ The Overgrowth—Fire
○ Trapping Pit—Fire
○ Tangled Thicket—Fire
○ Canopy Hot Springs—Water
○ Prickly Pastures—Life
○ Old Treetop Terrace—Earth
○ Honey Trove—Earth
○ Long Worn Hollow—Earth
○ Bulwark Overlook—Air
○ Canopy Cave—Earth
○ Gold Hewn Basin—Earth
○ Knotted Heights—Water
○ Woodburrow Landing—Water

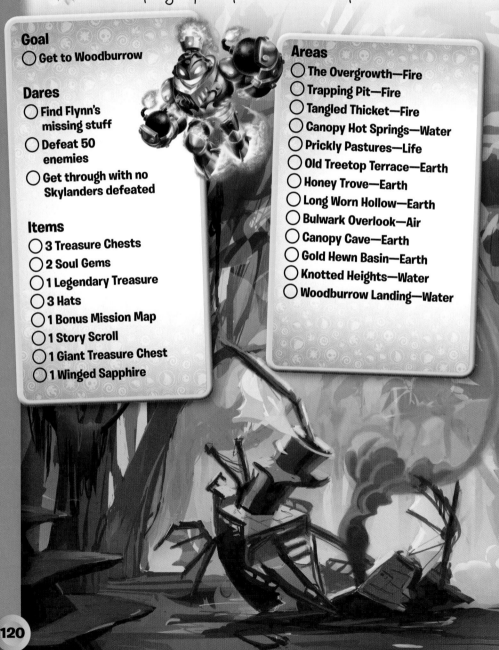

INTO THE VOLCANO

As Flynn flies through the volcano, be sure to clear the back of the ship of debris.

HINT: As you'll see, it's worth destroying anything you can—you never know what you'll discover.

Press X to Attack

CHOMPY BATTLE

Uh-oh! Greeble Sky Barons swoop in and drop a load of Chompies. Watch out for those teeth. It's good practice for the wave of Greebles coming in next!

HINT: Don't forget to grab all those energy orbs.

CRASH SITE

After Flynn pulls off his "super-secret incredibly complex maneuver" (otherwise known as a crash) you'll need to head to Woodburrow.

HINT: Before joining Tessa, head back the way you came to find the first of Flynn's missing stuff.

EON'S TIP
Your Skylanders can now jump, meaning they can leap over obstacles and explore higher ground.

THE OVERGROWTH

Head up onto the leaves to find Barkin trapped in a cage—it's just a shame you'll tumble into a Trapping Pit. Head into battle to open the Battle Gate.

HINT: You'll need to defeat all the Chompies for the Battle Gate to open.

TANGLED THICKET

Help Miss Poppy and the others get out of the cages by loosening the hooks. Once they're free, Miss Poppy will help the rest escape.

HINT: Before heading up to Miss Poppy, look behind the big rock for more of Flynn's missing stuff.

TANGLED THICKET

Grab the key and unlock the gate. You'll find two different Element Gates. Use Skylanders that match the symbols to open them up and explore inside.

HINT: Use the water jets to bounce up Canopy Hot Springs' water platforms and get your prize.

PRICKLY PASTURES

Little Bro Pete has lost his sheep. You'll need to defeat Lieutenant Woalf's Greeble Screwballs as you get them back.

HINT: Don't get stuck on any spikes. They glow before popping up.

OLD TREETOP TERRACE

You'll find block puzzles throughout the Cloudbreak Islands. Shove them forward to complete your path.

HINT: You can also use blocks to jump up to raised platforms ... which is how you'll reach one of the Soul Gems.

EXTRA

Flynn's missing fluffy dice are on an island to the right just after you find Pop Thorn's Soul Gem. There's a Story Scroll nearby, too.

OLD TREETOP TERRACE

Slide down the vines, jumping to grab extra coins on your way. You'll find shortcuts like this throughout your journey.

HINT: After you defeat the Chompy Pod, jump down to the left. There's a cave containing Magna Charge's Soul Gem and more of Flynn's secret stuff to find!

BULWARK OVERLOOK

Go through the Air Elemental Gate to help Wixxon with his cannon. Again, this is good training for later in the game, so take your time to get it right.

HINT: Destroy 50 Greeble Bombers to receive a Winged Sapphire.

EON'S TIP

Watch out for those missiles. You need to knock them out of the sky before they hit your gun turret.

LONG WORN HOLLOW

After the Elemental Gate, head down to the right to find a cave containing a Giant Chest.

HINT: There's more of Flynn's stuff by the entrance to the cave, but you'll need to find something to bridge the gap to reach it.

WOODBURROW LANDING

The Greebles are blocking the entrance to Woodburrow. Clear them to open the gate.

HINT: Destroy the Chompy Pods first to staunch the flow of Chompies.

CENTRAL PLAZA

Rufus the Village Crier welcomes you to Woodburrow. There are few tasks to complete before your journey continues. First, open the power pod for the Hipbros.

HINT: Need to get over to the airdocks? Use the jump pad as a shortcut.

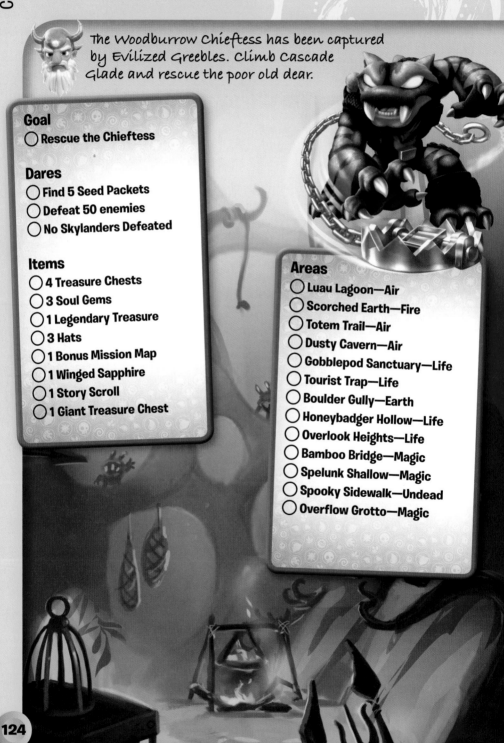

CHAPTER 2

CASCADE GLADE

The Woodburrow Chieftess has been captured by Evilized Greebles. Climb Cascade Glade and rescue the poor old dear.

Goal
○ Rescue the Chieftess

Dares
○ Find 5 Seed Packets
○ Defeat 50 enemies
○ No Skylanders Defeated

Items
○ 4 Treasure Chests
○ 3 Soul Gems
○ 1 Legendary Treasure
○ 3 Hats
○ 1 Bonus Mission Map
○ 1 Winged Sapphire
○ 1 Story Scroll
○ 1 Giant Treasure Chest

Areas
○ Luau Lagoon—Air
○ Scorched Earth—Fire
○ Totem Trail—Air
○ Dusty Cavern—Air
○ Gobblepod Sanctuary—Life
○ Tourist Trap—Life
○ Boulder Gully—Earth
○ Honeybadger Hollow—Life
○ Overlook Heights—Life
○ Bamboo Bridge—Magic
○ Spelunk Shallow—Magic
○ Spooky Sidewalk—Undead
○ Overflow Grotto—Magic

TOTEM TRAIL

Line up the blocks to make your way over to a leap pad that will shoot you up to meet Pollywog.

HINT: When you reach Gobblepod Sanctuary, free the Gobble Pods to get through the battle gate.

SCORCHED EARTH

Use a Fire Skylander to jump through the Elemental Gate, and then leap from one lava platform to the next to reach a Legendary Treasure.

HINT: After you've defeated the Evilized Greeble Blunderbusses, look out for a path to the right to find your first seed packet.

BOULDER GULLY

Use the push blocks to grab the two gears, then throw them into the mechanism at the back of the cave and hit the switch.

HINT: Keep your eyes out for a Stealth SWAP Challenge. Hide from the spotlights to win a Hat.

HONEYBADGER HOLLOW

Climb the steps to grab some treasure, then head back down to exit the cave.

HINT: Before opening the next Spark Lock, jump down and get another seed packet.

EXTRA

Listen for a chime when solving block puzzles. It means you've got it right.

Spooky Sidewalk

Get Skully's hat back from the Greebles. Smash your way through their defenses and return the stylish skullwear to the bonehead.

HINT: Keep an eye out for Seeker Scopes. They help you spy treasure on the path ahead. All that glitters is gold!

OVERFLOW GROTTO

Take out the waves of Greebles and Chompies to release the Chieftess.

HINT: Free the Gobble Pods as soon as you can. They'll eat your enemies for you.

CHAPTER 3

MUDWATER HOLLOW

 The Chieftess is safe, but Kaos has discovered where the four Ancient Elementals are hiding. He's trying to Evilize the ancient Flashfin. You need to stop him—and fast!

Goals
- ⭕ Get to the Ancient Flashfin
- ⭕ Catch 3 Piranhas
- ⭕ Catch the Gear Fish
- ⭕ Save the village
- ⭕ De-Evilize the Bog Hog
- ⭕ Destroy the crystals

Dares
- ⭕ Collect 6 Floaty Life Preservers
- ⭕ Defeat 50 enemies
- ⭕ No Skylanders defeated

Items
- ⭕ 6 Treasure Chests
- ⭕ 3 Soul Gems
- ⭕ 2 Legendary Treasures
- ⭕ 2 Hats
- ⭕ 1 Bonus Mission Map
- ⭕ 1 Winged Sapphire
- ⭕ 1 Story Scroll
- ⭕ 1 Giant Treasure Chest

Areas
- ⭕ Woodbridge Way—Air
- ⭕ Froghollow Fishin' Pond—Air
- ⭕ Snagglescale's Bungalow—Air
- ⭕ Billy's Bend—Air
- ⭕ Billy's Bend Storehouse—Air
- ⭕ Snagglescale Swamp—Air
- ⭕ Crystal Pond—Life
- ⭕ Quiet Time Shallows—Air
- ⭕ Lazy Lock Isles—Fire
- ⭕ Lazy Lock Isles Gatehouse—Fire
- ⭕ Lazy Lock—Fire
- ⭕ Boom Boom Water Way—Fire
- ⭕ Broken Bog Bay—Fire
- ⭕ Mysterious Magical Maze—Magic
- ⭕ Big Gill Water Mill—Fire
- ⭕ Broken Bog Bay Lock—Fire
- ⭕ Don's Baitshop—Fire
- ⭕ Rumblin' Rapids—Magic
- ⭕ Muddy Marsh Village—Tech
- ⭕ Jug Jamboree Inn—Tech
- ⭕ Muddy Marsh Secret—Tech
- ⭕ Saltytooth's Scrap Shop—Tech
- ⭕ Precious Ponds—Water
- ⭕ Chompy Chew Shortcut—Magic
- ⭕ Muddy Marsh River—Tech
- ⭕ Ancient Tree Terrace—Water

WOODBRIDGE WAY

Snagglescale the Gillman is having trouble with piranhas. Time to go fishing. Catch all three and he'll build you a bridge to cross the electric eel-infested water.

HINT: Keep your bobber away from whirlpools. Your fishing skills will come in handy later on at the Crystal Pond.

BILLY'S BEND

Shove the red-roofed huts into the gap to grab the key for the lock.

HINT: Drop the third hut into the hole to jump up to a treasure chest.

QUIET TIME SHALLOWS

Help Snagglescale pilot his boat by shifting your weight from left to right. Don't hit the mines if you want to stay out of the swim.

HINT: To get through Lazy Lock you'll need a spare gear from Salvage Steve. Shame it's been swallowed by a fish!

MUDDY MARSH VILLAGE

Clear the village of enemies to unlock the Magic Circle. It's a Portal that will blast you nearer to the Ancient Flashfin.

HINT: Clear garbage at the back of the jumping Jug Jamboree Inn to find a Soul Gem.

EXTRA
After de-Evilizing the Bog Hog, bear right. That way you can find another Soul Gem.

ANCIENT TREE TERRACE

Destroy the four crystals to save Flashfin. Be warned—all manner of enemies will descend on you as you do.

HINT: Even when destroying the crystals, keep an eye out. Can you spot one last Floaty Life Preserver?

CHAPTER 4

RAMPANT RUINS

 The robots buried in the Rampant Ruins graveyard were powered by petrified Darkness. Could this be where Kaos is creating his diabolical Evilizers?

Goals
- ⭘ De-Evilize the Sugarbats
- ⭘ Get to the Stone Monkey
- ⭘ Activate the Stone Monkey

Dares
- ⭘ Find 5 Grave Monkey Totems
- ⭘ Defeat 50 enemies
- ⭘ No Skylanders defeated

Items
- ⭘ 5 Treasure Chests
- ⭘ 2 Soul Gems
- ⭘ 2 Legendary Treasures
- ⭘ 2 Hats
- ⭘ 1 Bonus Mission Map
- ⭘ 1 Winged Sapphire
- ⭘ 1 Story Scroll
- ⭘ 1 Giant Treasure Chest

Areas
- ⭘ Iron Tomb Trail—Air
- ⭘ Mystic Flame Rotunda—Fire
- ⭘ Gibbon Antechamber—Life
- ⭘ Orangutan Tower—Life
- ⭘ Simian Temple—Fire
- ⭘ Simian Throne Room—Fire
- ⭘ Gibbon's Garden—Earth
- ⭘ Guardian's Lookout—Earth
- ⭘ Hidden Temple—Water
- ⭘ Western Watch—Earth
- ⭘ Monkey Monk's Path—Undead
- ⭘ Eastern Watch—Undead

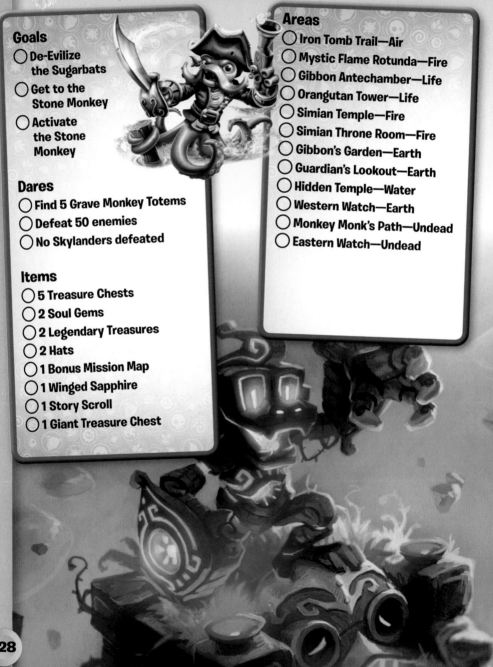

GIBBON ANTECHAMBER

Willowbark and his band of Ent Archaeologists are having trouble with Evilized Sugarbats. Blast them to save the dig.

HINT: Dodge the short-sighted bats and they'll crash into walls. Much easier to hit when they're dazed!

GIBBON ANTECHAMBER

Open the devious gate by hitting the switch when the rotating purple gems are perfectly lined up. Warning: The gates get even more devious after this one.

HINT: After heading down to Simian Temple, beat up on some bats before continuing for extra treasure.

ORANGUTAN TOWER

Climb the tower, avoiding the spikes. You can see when they're going to pop up. Just watch for the glow.

HINT: Be sure you want to enter the Superbat Arena. You'll get locked in as soon as you cross the threshold.

EXTRA

There's treasure to be had as you head down Guardian's Lookout. You'll have to find a gap in the railings.

WESTERN WATCH

You need to reactivate the Stone Guardian (aka the Grave Monkey). Stop the spinning gears by using the switch so that the light beam can get through.

HINT: After you've jumped over the monkey, keep your eye out for a Story Scroll.

EASTERN WATCH

Defeat the enemies to unlock the last two switches you need to activate the Grave Monkey.

HINT: You'll need to line up the gear with the yellow gems first for the beam to get through.

CHAPTER 5

JUNGLE RUMBLE

Just when you think the monkey has the upper paw, Evil Glumshanks knocks him flying with an Arkeyan tank. Teach that troll a lesson with this step-by-step guide.

~~Good~~ Bad old Glumshanks!

Glumshanks has been looking after Kaos ever since the evil Portal Master was a baby. The poor troll even had to change Kaos's diapers. Yuck!

He has remained loyal to his master through thick and thin (okay, there's definitely been more thin), but now that he's been Evilized he's taking out years of frustration and abuse—on you!

Goals

○ Defeat Evil Glumshanks
○ No Skylanders defeated
○ No damage taken

TROLL TANK

Glumshanks's tank is protected by magic. Trick the Evilized butler into driving it into the spikes.

HINT: Watch for the red target to see where he's heading.

AIM AND FIRE

Blast the tank when its armor is scattered around.

HINT: Hurry, he'll soon put it back together again!

CARELESS DRIVER

Glumshanks is no fool. He gets rid of some of the spikes—but not enough (so perhaps he is just a little bit of a fool, after all).

HINT: Use yourself as bait in front of the spikes.

TARGET PRACTICE

Kaos's bolstered butler starts summoning missiles from the heavens. Get out of their way.

HINT: The targets on the floor give you a clue to where they'll land.

MINION MENACE

Glumshanks has been taking hints from Kaos. He's summoned minions. Show them why Kaos always loses.

HINT: Use the last spikes to finish Glumshanks off.

131

CHAPTER 6

IRON JAW GULCH

Kaos is going after the Ancient Terrasquid. Travel to Iron Jaw Gulch to find Marshal Wheellock. He'll know the location of the tentacled one. But beware, Kaos has sent his pirate Greebles.

Goals
- ○ Destroy the Airships

Dares
- ○ Find 4 Marshal Wheellock plushies
- ○ Defeat 50 enemies
- ○ No Skylanders defeated

Items
- ○ 2 Treasure Chests
- ○ 3 Soul Gems
- ○ 2 Legendary Treasures
- ○ 2 Hats
- ○ 1 Bonus Mission Map
- ○ 1 Winged Sapphire
- ○ 1 Story Scroll
- ○ 1 Giant Treasure Chest

Areas
- ○ Iron Jaw Gulch—Magic
- ○ Cactus Pass—Magic
- ○ The Canteen—Magic
- ○ Impenetrable Fort—Magic
- ○ Sky Gear Gulch—Air
- ○ Huckster's Hutch—Fire
- ○ Sun-Smoked Strand—Fire
- ○ Cuddy's Cottage—Fire
- ○ Quaint Cottage—Fire
- ○ Iron Jaw Inn—Fire
- ○ Pump Station—Tech
- ○ 10,000 Gallon Hat—Undead
- ○ Kangarat Groove Hut
- ○ Grooving Gardens—Life
- ○ Okey Dokey Corral—Undead
- ○ Last Train West—Undead

CACTUS PASS

Some varmint has stolen the handle to the bridge mechanism. Head into The Canteen and deliver a beat that will get the Kangarats jumping. You'll need to hit all the drums to get them going.

HINT: It's best if you don't bump into any of the cacti—if you get my point.

SUN-SMOKED STRAND

Work your way around the Strand to meet a Land Shark who'll show you how to sink the pirate airships.

HINT: Take a bounce up to the top of Cuddy's Cottage for rich pickings.

GROOVING GARDENS

You have to bounce on all seven revolving drums to open the gates to the Bonus Mission Map.

HINT: The middle Ho-Down Square stays the right way up at all times. Use it as a safe haven during drum rolls.

EXTRA

Never try to jump on the Pump Station's rollers from below. You'll be sent spinning back.

OKEY DOKEY CORRAL

It's last chance corral for your enemies as you fight your way through to the end platform.

HINT: Blast all the water towers you can see. You never know what's hiding beneath.

LAST TRAIN WEST

You'll need to clear this area completely to blast the biggest airship of them all.

HINT: Treat the platform like an arena. Get into the ring of revolving mines and use a long-ranged Skylander to take out those enemies.

CHAPTER 7

MOTLEYVILLE

Wheellock didn't know where the Terrasquid was. Travel to the junkyards of Motleyville and track down Sharpfin. He knows everything. Let's just hope Baron von Shellshock, servant of Kaos, hasn't taken over the place. What's that? He has! You better stop him, then.

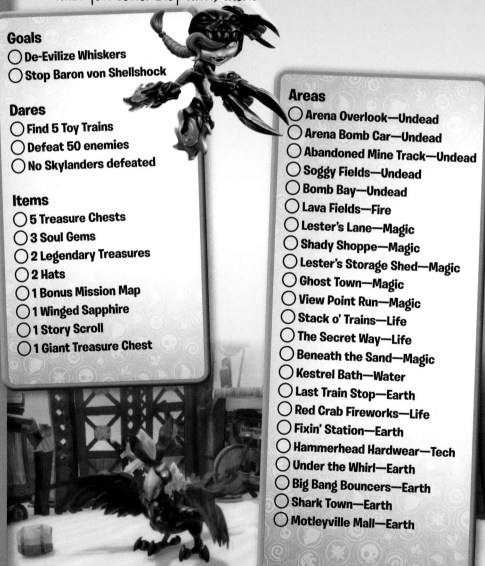

Goals
- ○ De-Evilize Whiskers
- ○ Stop Baron von Shellshock

Dares
- ○ Find 5 Toy Trains
- ○ Defeat 50 enemies
- ○ No Skylanders defeated

Items
- ○ 5 Treasure Chests
- ○ 3 Soul Gems
- ○ 2 Legendary Treasures
- ○ 2 Hats
- ○ 1 Bonus Mission Map
- ○ 1 Winged Sapphire
- ○ 1 Story Scroll
- ○ 1 Giant Treasure Chest

Areas
- ○ Arena Overlook—Undead
- ○ Arena Bomb Car—Undead
- ○ Abandoned Mine Track—Undead
- ○ Soggy Fields—Undead
- ○ Bomb Bay—Undead
- ○ Lava Fields—Fire
- ○ Lester's Lane—Magic
- ○ Shady Shoppe—Magic
- ○ Lester's Storage Shed—Magic
- ○ Ghost Town—Magic
- ○ View Point Run—Magic
- ○ Stack o' Trains—Life
- ○ The Secret Way—Life
- ○ Beneath the Sand—Magic
- ○ Kestrel Bath—Water
- ○ Last Train Stop—Earth
- ○ Red Crab Fireworks—Life
- ○ Fixin' Station—Earth
- ○ Hammerhead Hardwear—Tech
- ○ Under the Whirl—Earth
- ○ Big Bang Bouncers—Earth
- ○ Shark Town—Earth
- ○ Motleyville Mall—Earth

ABANDONED MINE TRACK

Quick! Follow Shellshock by slip-sliding on the mine track rails. Just make sure you leap from rail to rail to avoid the mines.

HINT: Don't sink into the slime pits at Soggy Fields.

BOMB BAY

You'll need to blast your way through the gates. Head into the hut to find explosives—but hurry, the dynamite only has a short fuse.

HINT: Head over the goop and jump the rocks to the right to find a vampire's Soul Gem.

LESTER'S LANE

Rubble is blocking your way into Ghost Town. Better get down to Gibbs—he's got a cannon waiting for you.

HINT: The dynamite you need to get to Gibbs is in the Shady Shoppe, but you'll have to fight for it.

EXTRA

Before continuing through to the Ghost Town, push the cannon back a bit to target another pile of junk.

THE SECRET WAY

Shellshock has Evilized Whiskers. Watch the targets on the floor to see where he is going to land.

HINT: Get the birdie every time its head is stuck in the sand.

MOTLEYVILLE MALL

Shellshock has been hiding his secret weapon—an enemy-slinging mechanical crustacean.

HINT: Grab the dynamite the Baron slings and chuck it back. Then hit him with everything you've got when Shellshock's down.

CHAPTER 8

TWISTY TUNNELS

Sharpfin is ready to rocket you off to find the Terrasquid. You just need to watch out for Kaos's Fire Viper of Doom.

Goals
- ○ Destroy the Evilizer Crystals
- ○ Get to the Ancient Terrasquid

Dares
- ○ Find 5 Rubber Duckies
- ○ Defeat 50 enemies
- ○ No Skylanders defeated

Items
- ○ 5 Treasure Chests
- ○ 3 Soul Gems
- ○ 2 Legendary Treasures
- ○ 2 Hats
- ○ 1 Bonus Mission Map
- ○ 1 Winged Sapphire
- ○ 1 Story Scroll
- ○ 1 Giant Treasure Chest

Areas
- ○ Mythic Mesa—Tech
- ○ Perilous Plateau—Tech
- ○ High in the Sky—Air
- ○ Crystal Crashing—Tech
- ○ Guardian Gangway—Tech
- ○ Sandy Cavern—Tech
- ○ Sandstone Secret—Tech
- ○ Arid Cave—Fire
- ○ Hazardous Highway—Fire
- ○ Energetic Evilizer—Fire
- ○ Underground Lake—Fire
- ○ Undead Uprising—Undead
- ○ Serene Walkway—Fire
- ○ Bounce Fountain—Water
- ○ Floating Foray—Magic
- ○ Catalytic Crystal—Magic

PERILOUS PLATEAU

The key to the gate is buried somewhere in the sand. Find the spade and follow the guides to know where to dig. "X" marks the spot.

HINT: Be prepared—you might also dig up some Chompies!

EXTRA

On Perilous Plateau, blast crates to find your way down to your first rubber ducky!

CRYSTAL CRASHING

Shrink down small enough to enter the first Evilizer crystal and smash it from the inside. Small is beautiful!

HINT: Avoid the electrified rods as you climb inside the crystal and unscrew its power supply. The ghastly gem will blow!

HAZARDOUS HIGHWAY

Look out! The Fire Viper has spewed fireballs all over the highway. Dodge them to get to the second crystal.

HINT: Before you start avoiding the fireballs, head down the path to the left to give Wash Buckler a helping tentacle.

BOUNCE FOUNTAIN

Rockgill's friends are stuck on the water shoots. Jump on the bounce pad to lower them to safety one leap at a time.

HINT: Once you've got your hat, leap left before talking to Sharpfin for the last ducky!

SERENE WALKWAY

Not so serene after all. Troll reinforcements are on the way. Knock them out of the sky with Sharpfin's sharkcannon.

HINT: Once you're done head up to the last crystal, avoiding the Fire Viper's breath. You'll be seeing more of him.

CHAPTER 9

SERPENT'S PEAK

You may have freed the Terrasquid, but Kaos's Fire Viper is still causing . . . well, chaos. Better extinguish those flames.

Goals
- ○ Defeat the Fire Viper
- ○ No Skylanders defeated
- ○ No damage taken

FIRE VIPERS

Kaos wanted a Fire Viper of Doom ever since he was a little megalomaniac. He loved his Hydra—of course he did—but evil Portal Masters through the ages have always coveted the super-sized sizzling snake. One day he hopes to get his grubby hands on a Sand Serpent, but he is secretly scared of the two-headed serpent.

Top tips for beating a Fire Viper
- ○ Look out for the targets on the floor. They'll tell you where it's going to strike.
- ○ Avoid its roaming fireballs at all cost.
- ○ Blast its Evilized crystals.

DID YOU KNOW?
Kaos once used the Hydra to destroy the Core of Light. The jerk!

TAKE THAT, SUCKER!

First up, you'll need to get to the crossbows to tether the Fire Viper down.

HINT: Avoid its fiery breath to stick suckers on the left and the right.

CRYSTAL CRUMBLE

When it's down, jump on the Fire Viper's head and start blasting those crystals. Sharpfin will be on hand to dispense some food if you need it.

PEEK-A-BOO!

Oh no! The viper's broken free and is hiding behind the Terrasquid's tentacles. Time to use those crossbows again.

HINT: Use the Terrasquid's tentacles as cover.

KEEP FIRING!

Keep going until all its crystals are shattered. But don't relax—the crystal-less viper will be feeling hungry!

HINT: Be warned–the serpent's mines don't vanish after detonating.

THE BELLY OF THE BEAST!

Don't worry if you get swallowed. It was all part of the plan. You just need to destroy the crystals in its belly.

HINT: Fire Geargolems are on the way, so watch out. They're enough to give anyone burning indigestion.

CHAPTER 10

BONEY ISLANDS

The Frost Elves may be able to help you find the Ancient Frosthound—but they're having a bit of trouble with cyclopses. Go with Sharpfin to the Boney Islands to find Avril, Captain of the Frost Elf Guard.

Goals
- Find Fossil Fuel
- Find More Fossil Fuel
- Help the Caravan escape
- Return to the Caravan

Dares
- Find 4 Museum Souvenirs
- Defeat 50 enemies
- No Skylanders defeated

Items
- 5 Treasure Chests
- 2 Soul Gems
- 2 Legendary Treasures
- 2 Hats
- 1 Bonus Mission Map
- 1 Winged Sapphire
- 1 Story Scroll
- 1 Giant Treasure Chest

Areas
- Frozen Fossil Lane
- Gift Boat Row—Water
- Frosty Enchantment—Life
- Relic Room—Water
- McElfy's Diode Shoppe—Water
- Curator's Office—Water
- Dusty Archives—Water
- Triassic Turns—Air
- Paleo Pass—Air
- Aurora Way—Magic
- Ticket Taker—Air
- Security Hutch—Air
- Amber Alley—Tech
- Glacial Gallery—Tech
- Granite Wing—Earth
- Fossil Frostway—Tech

FROZEN FOSSIL LAKE

Protect the caravan as you make your way through the Frost Elves' museum, shoving blocks out of the way.

HINT: After the first block, climb the rickety ramp to find some treasure.

GIFT BOAT ROW

The caravan has run out of fuel. Head up to the Curator's Office to find some more juice.

HINT: Find the key to continue on your way by lining up the prisms in McElfy's Diode Shoppe to trigger the light lock.

PALEO PASS

Oh no! You've been blasted from the caravan. You'll need to climb up Paleo Pass to rejoin Avril.

HINT: Can't work out how to get Dune Bug's Soul Gem? Perhaps you need to drop a block from above?

EXTRA
Don't rush through the Ticket Taker without exploring the hut to the right. You'll find a timed challenge within the Security Hutch.

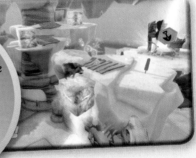

GRANITE WING

A winged sapphire hides behind those double gates. You'll need to swing the stone bridge to get from platform to platform.

HINT: Destroy all the enemies to gain access to the keys.

GLACIAL GALLERY

The bridge is under attack by Evilizer rays. Collect three keys by jumping on and off the revolving platforms to the left.

HINT: Once you've grabbed some fuel head back to the caravan, collecting more keys. Then, you'll need to destroy some dino-bones.

FOSSIL FROSTWAY

Take control of the caravan's cannons as you slide to the Frost Elves' ship.

HINT: Shoot mines and barriers to clear your way.

CHAPTER 11

WINTER KEEP

Avril's enchanted snow globe has revealed the blizzards of the Frostfest Mountains. The trouble is, no ship can navigate the storms. You'd better go find the Illuminator, a relic of the Frost Elves of Winter Keep. It will light your way . . .

Goals

- ○ Clear Out the South Wall
- ○ Thaw the Furnace
- ○ Defend the North Wall
- ○ Destroy all 3 Blizzard Bombers
- ○ Take back the Tower

Dares

- ○ Find 4 Lost Mittens
- ○ Defeat 50 enemies
- ○ No Skylanders defeated

Items

- ○ 4 Treasure Chests
- ○ 2 Soul Gems
- ○ 2 Legendary Treasures
- ○ 2 Hats
- ○ 1 Bonus Mission Map
- ○ 1 Winged Sapphire
- ○ 1 Story Scroll
- ○ 1 Giant Treasure Chest

Areas

- ○ The Blizzard Bridges—Tech
- ○ The Blue Ice Battlements
- ○ The Flame Steppes—Fire
- ○ Aurora Rails
- ○ The Snow Shovel in the Stone
- ○ Hidden Vault
- ○ The Frozen Curtain—Water
- ○ The Secret Keep—Water
- ○ Awestruck Orbits—Undead
- ○ Northern Light Rails
- ○ Frost Furnace
- ○ Hibernal Harbor
- ○ Sky Meadows—Air
- ○ Diamond Docks
- ○ Kaleidoscopic Kiln
- ○ Prism Tower—Earth

BLUE ICE BATTLEMENTS

Snowman the catapult and take out the first Blizzard Bomber.

HINT: The more you hit the bomber, the farther it'll retreat. You'll have to give your snowballs more power.

EXTRA

It's a little known fact that Snowrollers are extremely bouncy when you jump on them.

GUARDIAN OF THE SNOWSHOVEL
Sorry, Skylander. That is Snowscalibur! Only the truly worthy can draw it from the stone.

THE SNOW SHOVEL IN THE STONE

You need to get to the South Wall, but the key to the gate is lost in the snow. Can you pull Snowscalibur from the stone?

HINT: Dig to the left first to find a SWAP Challenge.

THE FROZEN CURTAIN

The Illuminator has been frozen! You need to get to the Aurora Rails. Climb to The Secret Keep and melt the ice that's blocking your way.

HINT: Drop the prism down from on high.

FROST FURNACE

Defeat the Ice Geargolem and then work the billows to defrost the furnace.

HINT: Next up, you'll need to gather snowmen to arm the catapults.

DIAMOND DOCKS

Use the blocks to position the prism on the revolving panel, then hit the switch to melt the ice and take out the remaining Blizzard Bombers.

HINT: It's not over yet. You'll need to get yourself to Prism Tower and defeat the last of Kaos's minions.

CHAPTER 12

FROSTFEST MOUNTAINS

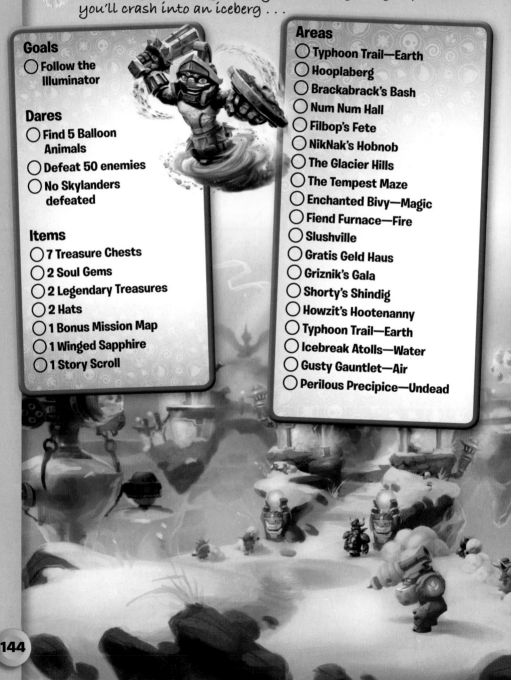

You have the Illuminator. Now you must quickly get to the Ancient Frosthound before Kaos! Just don't crash into an iceberg. Oh, hang on, Flynn is navigating. Of course you'll crash into an iceberg . . .

Goals
- ○ Follow the Illuminator

Dares
- ○ Find 5 Balloon Animals
- ○ Defeat 50 enemies
- ○ No Skylanders defeated

Items
- ○ 7 Treasure Chests
- ○ 2 Soul Gems
- ○ 2 Legendary Treasures
- ○ 2 Hats
- ○ 1 Bonus Mission Map
- ○ 1 Winged Sapphire
- ○ 1 Story Scroll

Areas
- ○ Typhoon Trail—Earth
- ○ Hooplaberg
- ○ Brackabrack's Bash
- ○ Num Num Hall
- ○ Filbop's Fete
- ○ NikNak's Hobnob
- ○ The Glacier Hills
- ○ The Tempest Maze
- ○ Enchanted Bivy—Magic
- ○ Fiend Furnace—Fire
- ○ Slushville
- ○ Gratis Geld Haus
- ○ Griznik's Gala
- ○ Shorty's Shindig
- ○ Howzit's Hootenanny
- ○ Typhoon Trail—Earth
- ○ Icebreak Atolls—Water
- ○ Gusty Gauntlet—Air
- ○ Perilous Precipice—Undead

TYPHOON TRAIL

Follow the light of the Illuminator through the blizzard until you get to Fizzy's lamp. You need to light it to banish the blizzard.

HINT: Stay and play some games in the village before heading up the mountain. Bozker will thank you!

THE TEMPEST MAZE

Leap through the gusts of the stone dogs to find treasure and scrolls.

HINT: Watch out for Mesmeralda's ticking time bombs. The ground goes red before they go off!

SLUSHVILLE

Blizzy wants you to play Volcano games to win himself some Yeti teddies. There's bobbing for apples (and mines), shuffle, and memory games.

HINT: There's a giant Treasure Chest to be found in one of these houses.

ICEBREAK ATOLLS

Cross the river by jumping from one ice floe to the next. Just don't hang around—they won't take your weight for long.

HINT: Take out the enemies on the way so that they don't knock you into the drink.

PERILOUS PRECIPICE

Before you head across the bridge to Perilous Precipice, head down between two snow-covered trees and jump across to a Soul Gem.

HINT: It's a case of one leap forward, two leaps back if you want to avoid Mesmeralda's exploding puppets.

Defeat the frosty foes at the top of the mountain to unlock the enemy gate that will let you light the final lamp.

HINT: Don't sit back on your laurels—the Frosthound isn't safe yet.

EXTRA

Want one large Treasure Chest before you reach the summit? Then wander off to the left as you climb the path.

145

CHAPTER 13

MESMERALDA'S SHOW

Mesmeralda loves to put on a show. But her pesky puppet chorus can leave you tangled in her deadly web. Don't be lulled by her song and dance number—her routines will slay you!

Sing-a-long-a-Mesmeralda

Lights in the house are dimming,
Prepared for the beginning,
Skylander come and take your seat,
All the voices hushing,
As the curtain's climbing,
Now, your eyes are fixed on ME!

Run to your mark, my pretties,
And to your place, my puppets,
Paint on your grins, no time to frown,
I have arrived to claim,
More than my share of fame,
For one night only in your town!

CHORUS

Make you laugh and then I'll make you cry,
Twist and tangle in my power,
All my enemies will cower,
Stand entranced as my fingers dance,
Captivated when I sing,
I'm the one who pulls your strings!
I'm the one who pulls your strings!

The dancers move with fury,
Their costumes all a flurry,
The music building to a roar,
I got you locked in knots,
Ya really have no shot,
Cause I'm the one who's keeping score!

Hold your breath, my dearie,
We're racing to finale,
A triple threat, my name's in lights,
Rise up now from your seat,
It's time for your defeat,
And we are lookin' for a fight!

Goals
- ○ Defeat Mesmerelda
- ○ No Skylanders defeated
- ○ No damage taken

OPENING NUMBER

Time for the first act. Don't let the puppet chorus mow you down.

HINT: Make sure you stay within their lines before they take to the stage.

GLARE OF THE SPOTLIGHT

Two searchlights will appear in the stands. Use them to blind Mesmeralda and then blast her before the bulbs smash.

HINT: If the first lamp you try doesn't find her, use the other one.

CLEARING THE THEATER

Talk about bombing on stage. The puppets are back, but this time Mesmeralda has added explosive ushers. This round's sure to be a smash hit.

HINT: Stay out of the red circles.

A LIGHT ATTACK

Put Mesmeralda under the spotlight once again—giving the bombs a wide berth as you do.

HINT: You'll have to avoid the ushers as you beat Mesmeralda.

THE THIRD ACT

Mesmeralda sends in spinning dancers. Leap over those blades.

HINT: Try to stay on the opposite side of the stage.

THE GRAND FINALE

Mesmeralda is throwing everything she's got at you. Find the light that will dazzle her and finish her off. The show must not go on.

HINT: Can you go back and get through Mesmeralda's Show without taking any damage at all?

CHAPTER 14

FANTASM FOREST

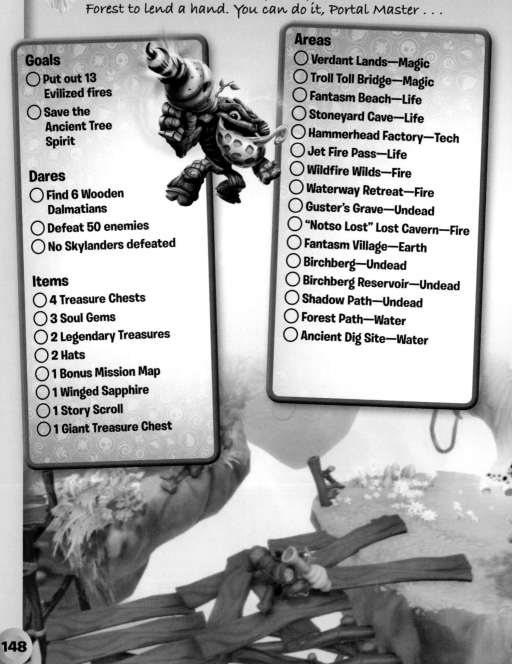

Three of the Ancient Elementals have returned to Woodburrow. The Tree Spirit is ready to join them, but has come under attack from Kaos and his force of Fire Trolls. Head to Fantasm Forest to lend a hand. You can do it, Portal Master . . .

Goals
- ○ Put out 13 Evilized fires
- ○ Save the Ancient Tree Spirit

Dares
- ○ Find 6 Wooden Dalmatians
- ○ Defeat 50 enemies
- ○ No Skylanders defeated

Items
- ○ 4 Treasure Chests
- ○ 3 Soul Gems
- ○ 2 Legendary Treasures
- ○ 2 Hats
- ○ 1 Bonus Mission Map
- ○ 1 Winged Sapphire
- ○ 1 Story Scroll
- ○ 1 Giant Treasure Chest

Areas
- ○ Verdant Lands—Magic
- ○ Troll Toll Bridge—Magic
- ○ Fantasm Beach—Life
- ○ Stoneyard Cave—Life
- ○ Hammerhead Factory—Tech
- ○ Jet Fire Pass—Life
- ○ Wildfire Wilds—Fire
- ○ Waterway Retreat—Fire
- ○ Guster's Grave—Undead
- ○ "Notso Lost" Lost Cavern—Fire
- ○ Fantasm Village—Earth
- ○ Birchberg—Undead
- ○ Birchberg Reservoir—Undead
- ○ Shadow Path—Undead
- ○ Forest Path—Water
- ○ Ancient Dig Site—Water

VERDANT LANDS

The Fire Trolls are setting fire to the forest. Connect the hose to Sprucie's pump and fill water balloons to put out the flames.

HINT: Go back and extinguish the blaze beside Sharpfin's boat for a soulful surprise.

EXTRA

Can you spot the first Wooden Dalmatian near Nolan? You'll have to bound over to this toy puppy.

FANTASM BEACH

Gillmen are on hand to lend a fin. Head into the cave to find a water hydrant and help douse the burning barges.

HINT: Don't rush on. Head back to find a SWAP Challenge and maybe even another Dalmatian.

JET FIRE PASS

Those flamethrowers will get you hot under the collar. Watch the balloons to see when they're going to go off.

HINT: Next up, you'll need to jump on board the fire flooder and put out flames as you go.

FANTASM VILLAGE

Foreverspring Village is on fire. Jump on the fire flooder to put out the blaze. The only snag this time is that you've got Missile Maulers taking pot shots at you too!

HINT: Take out the trolls first and then you can worry about the fires in the North and South villages.

ANCIENT DIG SITE

The flames are getting far too near the Ancient Tree Spirit. Douse them—and the trolls, too!

HINT: Once the fires are out, you need to turn your water cannon on Kaos himself. Block his missiles and try to extinguish his rocket boosters.

That's it! The Ancients are safe! The Cloudbreak Eruption Ceremony can begin. What can go wrong now? Oh—Kaos's mother, that's what!

CHAPTER 15

KAOS'S FORTRESS

 Kaos's mother has taken new Chieftess Tessa, but never fear . . . Flynn is standing by with his new improved Dread-Yacht. Hurry, we have an agent inside Kaos's Fortress to help.

Goals
- ○ Destroy the Sheepshooters

Dares
- ○ Find 4 Wool Sweaters
- ○ Defeat 50 enemies
- ○ No Skylanders defeated

Items
- ○ 6 Treasure Chests
- ○ 2 Soul Gems
- ○ 2 Legendary Treasures
- ○ 1 Hat
- ○ 2 Bonus Mission Maps
- ○ 1 Winged Sapphire
- ○ 1 Story Scroll
- ○ 1 Giant Treasure Chest

Areas
- ○ Liquid Goo Lab—Life
- ○ Contraption Lab—Life
- ○ Top Secret Storage—Life
- ○ Sheep Inspection—Life
- ○ Experimental Storage—Life
- ○ Sheep Tower—Life
- ○ Chompy's Last Stand
- ○ Glob Lobber Gangway—Air
- ○ Belly Flop Peak—Air
- ○ Chompie Churners—Air
- ○ Secret Testing Grounds—Air
- ○ Sludge Security—Tech
- ○ Dumping Grounds—Earth
- ○ Flooded Compartments—Tech
- ○ Mystical Fountains—Water
- ○ The Gauntlet—Tech
- ○ The Goo Pit of Doom
- ○ Sheeplight Checkout—Tech
- ○ Goo Pond—Magic
- ○ Super Duper Guardpost—Tech

LIQUID GOO LAB

Softpaw has gotten you into the Fortress. Jump over the gears, avoiding the goo as you go, to grab the key.

HINT: There's treasure to be found as you meet the K-Bot Gloopgunner.

EXTRA
If you see a lake of goo, move nearer—stepping stones may pop up!

SHEEP INSPECTION

Eye in the Sky Bots will remove anything that isn't a sheep. Grab a disguise from Softpaw and get across the grid.

HINT: Climb some steps to find a Soul Gem (while disguised as a sheep, that is!).

SHEEP TOWER

Solve the windy Spark Lock to blow the gun turret.

HINT: After surfboarding to safety, head left and up to find a Soul Gem and a chance to high-dive.

CHOMPIE CHURNERS

Make your way across the Churners, avoiding the goo and taking every opportunity to explore whenever you can jump off the blades.

HINT: Don't be too quick to climb the stairs. Head left first for a secret scroll and more!

SHEEPLIGHT CHECKPOINT

Avoiding the Eyes in the sky, grab the key and get through the gate. Like it or not, it's back in the sheep costume for your Skylander.

HINT: Prepare yourself for battle. You've got an arena to defeat before you bring down the final Sheepshooter.

CHAPTER 16

MOTHERLY MAYHEM

If you thought Kaos was bad, you ain't seen anything yet. His mother taught him everything he knows—and quite a lot he's forgotten. Head to the fortress to rescue Tessa from her clutches!

Goals
○ Defeat Kaos's mom
○ No Skylanders defeated
○ No damage taken

WANTED!
KAOS'S MOM

For capturing Tessa, being a ridiculously evil Portal Master, AND for having Kaos in the first place!

REWARD:
The safety of Skylands

CAGED ANIMALS

Kaos's mom releases her beasts from their cages. Quickly, take them out as quickly as you can.

HINT: Grab as much food as you can. This is going to be a long battle!

HIDE AND SEEK

Kaos's mother vanishes. Where has she gone? Is this really the time to play hide-and-seek?

HINT: Why not try taking your Skylander off your Portal?

DEFENDING CHAMPIONS

Head to the second arena after she escapes. You'll need to use all the skills you've learned defeating her defenders.

HINT: Remember how you found her last time she disappeared?

INSTANT DARKNESS

She's back—and she's zapping you with energy-sapping Darkness.

HINT: Kaos's mom's projectiles need to collide with the crystals.

ENTER BUBBA GREEBS

On to the third arena, avoiding the bouncing balls of goo! Look out! Bubba Greebs will throw minions and bombs from on high.

HINT: Why not throw one of those ticking bombs back at the big purple lump?

HIT HIM WHEN HE'S DOWN

Knock Bubba down from his perch and blast him when he's on the ground. Just make sure you're quick because he won't stay there for long.

HINT: Watch out for the shockwave as Bubba Greebs belly flops down.

MOM'S FINAL STAND

Tessa drops a handy mirror—although there's no time to reflect on what to do.

HINT: Jump on the mirror before Kaos's mother takes her shot.

Congratulations. You've defeated Kaos's mom. That's it. Adventure over. There wouldn't be one last challenge, would there? Turn the page and find out . . .

CHAPTER 17

CLOUDBREAK CORE

While you were dealing with his mother, Kaos was packing the Cloudbreak Volcano with petrified Darkness. He's planning to transform it into his biggest Evilizer ever. Even worse, he's been transformed into a huge, horrible version of himself (and let's face it—he was pretty bad before!).

Goals
- Defeat Super Evil Kaos
- No Skylanders defeated
- No damage taken

PUTTING HIS FOOT DOWN

Super Evil Kaos will try to stomp on you with his super evil feet. Avoid getting splatted at all costs.

HINT: Clip those crystallized toenails.

TONGUE TWISTER

Ugh! The oversized Portal Master tries to swallow you. Clean his teeth of crystals from within.

HINT: Prepare for a tussle on his terrible tongue, when Kaos throws a little golem and Chompy snacks.

BRAIN POWER

Kaos has got something on his mind. You! He's about to think up some big baddies to battle in his brain.

HINT: Glumshanks's tank is first. Wait for him to drop from the platform.

MIND FULL OF MINIONS

Next is a wave of trolls and Grumblebum Thrashers. Dodge in and out, taking them down one by one.

HINT: Kaos's brain will start throwing crystals at you. Destroy them one, two, three.

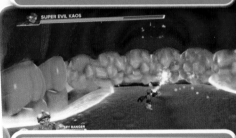

EYE EYE!

Next comes a cyclops attack. Take out the Gazermages first, then deal with the Arkeyan Rip-Rotors.

HINT: Kaos will start thinking about airships. Smash the crystals before he puts his mind to creating them!

THAT'S BAAAAD!

It's the stuff of nightmares. Sheep with Kaos faces. Don't tell Hugo about this—he won't sleep for months.

HINT: The loathsome lambs are easy to send wool-packing. Just hit them as they bounce!

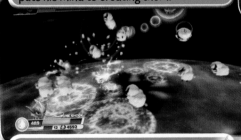

LOCK AND LOAD

Look! There's an ancient Arkeyan weapon. It might be able to defeat Kaos. Get to it quick—and then, as Flynn would say, "BOOM!"

HINT: Leap over Kaos's rays of pure Darkness as you go!

Mission completed! Well done, Portal Master. Kaos is defeated, Skylands is safe once again and it's all thanks to you. Now, come back to Woodburrow and see what Rufus has in store for you.

AFTER THE ADVENTURE

CHAMPION'S CHALLENGES

Your quest may be over, but the challenges of Skylands continue. Return to Woodburrow to discover some old friends and new challenges . . .

HINT
Keep a look out for shield tokens to protect you in battles.

SCORE MODE CHALLENGE

Head toward the Under Hollow and you'll bump into Wheellock, who has a new challenge for you. Go back and work your way through the chapters again, this time trying to beat the Star Scores.

THE MULTIPLIER

Fill the multiplier bar to double your score. Or triple, quadruple or quintuple, it, for that matter. Keep going and you can ramp it up to 10x!

TIME ATTACK

How speedy have you become? Avril is ready to test you to your limits. She's placed a timer on every chapter. Head back to see if you can beat the clock. Don't get distracted, as there's no time to lose.

HINT

Watch out for clock tokens. These handy timepieces will freeze the clock. The more you collect, the more time you can save.

159

BONUS MISSIONS

Visit my spirit in Woodburrow for the bonus missions you collected throughout your quest, Portal Master. They're trickier than you think . . .

CURSED STATUES

Destroy the cursed Arkeyan statues and the vile Greeble Corruptors they have attracted.

HINT: Ignore other enemies whenever you can.

EGG ROYALE

Return the Queen Turtle's eggs to the royal nest.

HINT: Beware: You'll drop your egg if you're hit!

FISHY FISHING

Stop the Greebles from harpooning Elder Fish by blowing up their wicked weapons.

HINT: It's easier to leap across the rolling barrel-ways.

CHOMPY CHALLENGE

Teleport from one part of the dig to the next, clearing Chompy Pods as you go. Just beware—some of the teleporters are traps.

HINT: Don't be too hasty destroying the pods. You need Chompies to beat.

CHOMPY SAUCE

Close the sauce valves to stop the Greebles from pumping Chompy Sauce into the Elder Fish's water.

HINT: Keys to locked gates will appear after battles.

FRIGID FRIGHT

Collect the elf ghosts and return them to the correct Portal.

HINT: You can only carry ghosts of one color at a time.

FROZEN DELIGHTS

Direct prism lasers to free the Yeti Elders trapped in piles of ice cream.

HINT: Don't wait around to fight enemies.

FRUIT FIGHT

Free the archaeologists from the middle of the Greebles' food fight by collecting the fruit.

HINT: Use the pumpkins to destroy the fruit crates.

GHOST TRAPS

Use bombs to free the wandering ghosts from their cyclops traps.

HINT: Defeating certain enemies will get you to different bombs.

GOLEM INVASION

Rescue the turtles from every kind of golem there is.

HINT: Look out for Spell Punks hiding behind barriers.

161

MAGIC CELLS

Collect the blue cells to recharge the Kangarats' power plant.

HINT: Avoid the red ones at all costs. Oh, and the air mines and laser beams, too!

MASTER CHEF

Fight your way through the Greeble hordes to get to the head chef before he serves up the Elder Fish.

HINT: Watch out for falling pumpkins!

PLANTS VS. CAKES

Feed the Greebles' celebratory cakes to the Gobble Pods. That'll ruin their party.

HINT: Watch the spikes to see when they're going to pop up.

ROYAL GEMS

Defeat Armored Cyclopses to retrieve the Frost Elves' stolen gems.

HINT: Take out the Spell Punks who are protecting the cyclopses.

SERPENT ATTACK

Search for magic flutes to put the three heads of the giant snake to sleep.

HINT: Look for boxes with magical notes.

SLEEPY TURTLES

Shove the sleeping turtle mamas back to their nests, clearing blocks and Chompy Pods out of their way.

HINT: Stone blocks squash Chompy Pods.

SWEET BLIZZARD

Destroy the cyclops's ice cream machines to stop the Yetis' home being covered in frozen desserts.

HINT: Don't get distracted by shiny baubles. Keep your mind on the task at hand.

THIEF ON THE RUN

Grab all the packages stolen by the Package Thieves.

HINT: Look for a Greeble with a red sack. That's the thief!

TREBLE THEFT

Retrieve the Kangarats' magical music instruments from the music-hating trolls.

HINT: Get the instruments back to the musicians to open the gates.

UNDERCOVER GREEBLES

Discover the Greebles in sheep's clothing and stop them from making off with the archaeologist's treasure.

HINT: Blast as many sheep as you can, just to make sure.

TOWER OF TIME

My Adventure Packs give you brand-new chapters—
and villains, too. Take Cluck, for example. This
calamitous chicken has invaded Clock Town. Time
itself is in danger!

Goals
- ○ Place three gears in the Town Center
- ○ Find the gear in the Steam Works
- ○ Find the gear in the Wind Works
- ○ Find the gear in the Water Works
- ○ Enter the Tower and defeat Cluck

Dares
- ○ Find 3 Tool Boxes
- ○ Defeat 50 enemies
- ○ No Skylanders defeated

Items
- ○ 3 Treasure Chests
- ○ 3 Legendary Treasures
- ○ 2 Hats
- ○ 1 Bonus Mission Map
- ○ 2 Winged Sapphires
- ○ 1 Story Scroll
- ○ 1 Giant Treasure Chest

Areas
- ○ Times Circle
- ○ Steam Works
- ○ Rickard's Gear—Tech
- ○ Wind Works—Air
- ○ Windianapolis—Air
- ○ Water Works—Water
- ○ Mount Clockmore
- ○ Tower of Time—Magic

TIMES CIRCLE

Use the time switch to freeze time just at the point that the steam bridge is raised.

HINT: Hit the trolls before they unfreeze!

STEAM WORKS

You'll have to use a combination of Time Switches and pistons to get to the top of the Steam Works and find the gear for the clock.

HINT: Hit the steam control and then freeze time to get to the pistons.

WIND WORKS

This is a block puzzle with a difference. As soon as you shove a block one way, huge fans blow it back.

HINT: Use the time switches to freeze the blocks where you need them.

EXTRA

After you've got the second gear, Cluck attacks. Time for those Time Switches again!

WATER WORKS

This time you'll have to open water valves to send barges across the depths.

HINT: Once again, freeze time when you have one or two barges lined up as a bridge.

TOWER OF TIME

Cluck has got himself another troll suit. Wait until he's crash-landed, and then freeze time.

HINT: Watch out for the Time Spell Punks. They'll unfreeze time just when you need it frozen.

SHEEP WRECK ISLANDS

The Sheep Mage (cousin to the equally annoying Chompy Mage) wants to turn everyone into sheep—starting with Flynn. Snap his source of power.

Goals
○ Destroy the Sheep Mage's staff

Dares
○ Find 3 Golden Sheep
○ Defeat 50 enemies
○ No Skylanders defeated

Items
○ 3 Treasure Chests
○ 3 Legendary Treasures
○ 3 Hats
○ 1 Bonus Mission Map
○ 2 Winged Sapphires
○ 1 Story Scroll
○ 1 Giant Treasure Chest

Areas
○ Sheepy Shores
○ Blind Beard's Ship—Undead
○ Ancient Ruins—Undead
○ Cyclops Ship—Undead
○ Temple Islands
○ Temple of Wool
○ Arr-Sheep—Elagos
○ Itchy Caves
○ Ram Galley
○ Woolly Caves—Earth
○ Old Sheep Cliff—Life
○ Temple of Baaaaa—Life
○ Altar of Worsheep

SHEEPY SHORES

Keep an eye out for the golden vortex. It'll send you spinning into a black hole— which is handy for getting across gaps.

HINT: There's a Treasure Chest after the second vortex.

ANCIENT RUINS

You need to grab the three keys from the Sheep Mage. Watch out! He's full of hot air.

HINT: Avoid the spiny creatures in the sand. Ouch!

TEMPLE ISLANDS

Defeat the Vortex Geargolem to open the door to the Temple of Wool.

HINT: Inside the temple, use the push blocks to jump higher.

EXTRA

There's a Winged Sapphire hidden in a gift box inside the Temple of Wool.

TEMPLE OF BAAAAA

Use sliding blocks to get across the ledge, avoiding mines and the Sheep Mage's baaad breath.

HINT: Statues provide good cover.

ALTAR OF WORSHEEP

Time to take out that woolly wizard. Blind Beard is on hand with some timed bombs.

HINT: Attack the staff every time the Sheep Mage is suffering.

BATTLE ARENAS

POWER-UPS

Throughout the battles and arena modes, keep your eyes peeled for some handy power-ups.

STORM IN A BOTTLE

Unleash a cloudy curse on your opponent.

POOKY

Enlist an Evilized Sugarbat to attack from above.

ICE SHIELD

Give your enemies a frosty reception with these defenses.

TWIN ROCKETS

Speed up your attacks with a little turbo boost.

MAGNIFIER

Burn your enemies with rays magnified through a lens.

ENTER THE ARENA

Arena battles help you train your Skylanders. There are five main modes—some for you to struggle through on your own, others where you can enlist the services of your friends. Then, when you've worked together, you can try to destroy each other! Just be careful. Kaos used to gloat after Battle Arena victories, and look at what happened to him . . .

FAIR PLAY!

The more experience your Skylanders have, the more powerful they become. However, if you want to give each opponent an equal chance, head to the match settings and select "Fair Fight."

Here you'll also be able to choose whether food or power-ups are available throughout the bout. Each competitor is automatically given one life in a battle. Why not make your clash truly epic by upping that to three, five, seven, or even nine?

THE FIVE BATTLE MODES

SOLO SURVIVAL

Work your way through Snagglescale's arenas, defeating wave after wave of enemies.

TEAM SURVIVAL

Two Portal Masters are better than one. Take Snagglescale's challenges together.

RIVAL SURVIVAL

Enter Snaggescale's arenas and try to earn more points than your rivals.

BATTLE ARENA

The gloves are off (and, in the case of zombies, the hands, too). Use the hazards to help defeat other Portal Masters.

RING OUT

Knock your rivals out of the arena. Throw everything you have at them.

SOLO SURVIVAL

Visit Snagglescale in Woodburrow to keep your skills sharp with his arena challenges.

SUPER HUNGRY GOBBLE PODS

Release the Gobble Pods from their cages while fighting three waves of rampaging enemies.

HINT: Stop the Food Thief between stages to release loads of health-boosting grub.

POKEY POKEY SPIKES

Blast your enemies while avoiding the spikes. Shame that cloud curse is zapping your strength as you go.

HINT: Don't be tempted to eat all the food at once. Save some for when you need it most.

ANGRY ANGRY PLANTS

Have you ever seen so many enemies in one arena? All you've got to do is wipe 'em out. Easy, eh?

HINT: Get rid of the Chompy Pods first to cut down the number of teeth trying to bite you.

CHOMP CHOMP CHOMPIES

Protect the Grave Monkey's fruit offering. Hungry mouths will be coming at you from all angles.

HINT: Use a Skylander with a long-range weapon so you can stay near the fruit at all times.

SAND-PIT-FALL

Defeat three waves of enemies, while trying to trick them into the sinking sand pit in the middle of the arena.

HINT: Watch out for the magnifying glass power-up. It'll help fry your foes.

SHELLSHOCK'S CURSE

It's back to the sandpit, but this time you're cursed. Get those enemies into the sinkhole before your energy completely runs out.

HINT: Cornered? Then jump into the sinkhole yourself. You'll be teleported away from your enemies.

BEWARE OF THE BIRD

The minions are the least of your worries. Watch out for the giant Evilized bird.

HINT: Jump over the feathered fury's shockwaves.

SNAKE IN THE HOLE

Take out the snake as you fight your way through enemies.

HINT: Play the magic flute to send the slippery serpent to sleep!

BOARDING PARTY

Enemies are boarding your icy ship. Wipe them off the poop deck.

HINT: You can always try shoving them overboard, too!

ICICLE BOMBING

Avoid the ice cannons while cursed. Getting hit will just slow you down.

HINT: Keep bashing enemies—they'll spawn all-important food.

EXTRA

Every time you're hit, you lose points on your multiplier.

EXTRA

Farther Survival Challenges can be unlocked using the Sheep Wreck Island and Arkeyan Crossbow statues.

EXPLODING SNOWMEN

Stay clear of Mesmeralda's exploding ice bombs to get through this challenge.

HINT: You don't want to get caught in the snowmen's red rings.

PERFECT CAPTAIN

This is the trickiest arena challenge of all. One hit and you're out!

HINT: This isn't a battle for close combat. Use a Skylander who can blast from afar.

THE ARENAS

Friendship means nothing when the Skylanders meet in battle. Why not challenge another Portal Master to an arena campaign? Pit your favorite Skylanders against each other. May the best Portal Master win!

RAMPART RUINS

Duke it out on the top of two crumbling towers as Greebles watch. There's nowhere to run, so you'll need to meet your opponent head on. Try to ram them into the floating air mines or leap to safety using the two teleporters.

QUICKSAND QUARRY

Try to stay out of the sand as you fight. Get a sinking feeling and you'll find yourself falling off the edge of the island. There's a couple of Bounce Pads for leaping to safety, and you may be able to use those spiky cacti to your advantage.

FROZEN OUTPOST

Cyclopses cheer as you clash in a chilly coliseum. The teleporters beam you up high, but be careful if you try to transport back down. You'll end up in the middle of the spike pit. You don't want your opponent to jump on any three of those spike switches!

HINT

If you're lucky, you'll be given a bomb to throw. Just don't wait too long.

FIERY FORGE

You need the Fiery Forge figure to unlock this arena. Battle over or around three red-hot lava pits. Just beware of bubbling lakes of lava rising from the floor. It fills each of the pits in turn.

TREACHEROUS BEACH

Drop the Arkeyan Crossbow statue onto your Portal to unlock this arena. Duke it out from the top of two sandcastles, using the two Bounce Pads to send yourself soaring through the air.

RING OUT ARENAS

Ring the changes in the extra Ring Out Arenas!

Quick Draw Corral

Punch your opponent over the low walkway.

Blossom Islands

The wooden walkways are an ideal place to attack.

Tic Toc Terrace

Spinning cogs and gears are always on the move.

HINT

Unlock Tic Toc Terrace with the Tower of Time Adventure Pack.

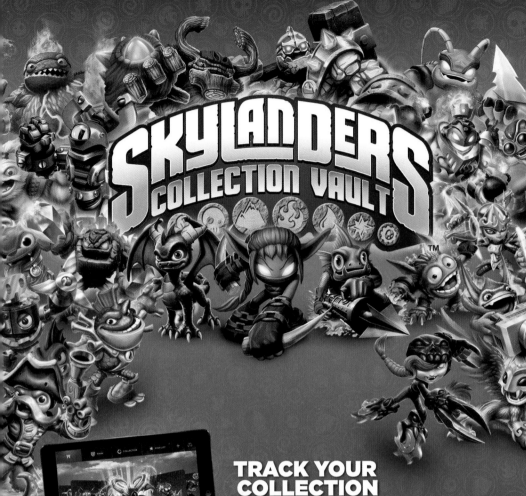

SKYLANDERS
COLLECTION VAULT

™

**TRACK YOUR
COLLECTION
AND LEVEL UP**

SPYRO

WISH LIST 15

**CREATE
AND SHARE
YOUR WISH LIST**

**DOWNLOAD
THE FREE APP**

Download on the
App Store